Cambridge Elements

Elements in Publishing and Book Culture
edited by
Samantha J. Rayner
University College London
Leah Tether
University of Bristol

INCLUSIVE PUBLISHING AND THE QUEST FOR READING EQUITY

Agata Mrva-Montoya
University of Sydney

Shaftesbury Road, Cambridge CB2 8EA, United Kingdom

One Liberty Plaza, 20th Floor, New York, NY 10006, USA

477 Williamstown Road, Port Melbourne, VIC 3207, Australia

314–321, 3rd Floor, Plot 3, Splendor Forum, Jasola District Centre, New Delhi – 110025, India

103 Penang Road, #05–06/07, Visioncrest Commercial, Singapore 238467

Cambridge University Press is part of Cambridge University Press & Assessment, a department of the University of Cambridge.

We share the University's mission to contribute to society through the pursuit of education, learning and research at the highest international levels of excellence.

www.cambridge.org
Information on this title: www.cambridge.org/9781009528474

DOI: 10.1017/9781009528511

© Agata Mrva-Montoya 2025

This publication is in copyright. Subject to statutory exception and to the provisions of relevant collective licensing agreements, no reproduction of any part may take place without the written permission of Cambridge University Press & Assessment.

When citing this work, please include a reference to the DOI 10.1017/9781009528511

First published 2025

A catalogue record for this publication is available from the British Library

ISBN 978-1-009-52847-4 Paperback
ISSN 2514-8524 (online)
ISSN 2514-8516 (print)

Cambridge University Press & Assessment has no responsibility for the persistence or accuracy of URLs for external or third-party internet websites referred to in this publication and does not guarantee that any content on such websites is, or will remain, accurate or appropriate.

For EU product safety concerns, contact us at Calle de José Abascal, 56, 1°, 28003 Madrid, Spain, or email eugpsr@cambridge.org

Inclusive Publishing and the Quest for Reading Equity

Elements in Publishing and Book Culture

DOI: 10.1017/9781009528511
First published online: July 2025

Agata Mrva-Montoya
University of Sydney

Author for correspondence: Agata Mrva-Montoya, agata.mrva-montoya@sydney.edu.au

ABSTRACT: Despite unprecedented opportunities to publish content in accessible formats, most books remain inaccessible to people with print disability. Technological advances and new legal frameworks are creating a transition towards inclusive publishing practices, but systemic barriers continue to limit equitable access to books for millions of individuals worldwide. Scholarship has also moved slowly, leaving a significant gap in our understanding of the strategic, technological, and ethical dimensions of inclusive publishing. This Element offers the first holistic examination of this landscape, and argues for the need to move away from ad hoc remediation of books towards the commercial production of 'born-accessible' content. Through policy research, industry case studies, and strategic partnership mapping, it critically examines the rationale, implementation, and potential of inclusive publishing. By articulating both business imperatives and social responsibilities, it proposes a transformative framework for understanding accessibility that offers valuable insights for researchers, industry professionals, and advocacy groups.

KEYWORDS: accessibility, print disability, inclusive publishing, accessible publishing, born-accessible publication

© Agata Mrva-Montoya 2025

ISBNs: 9781009528474 (PB), 9781009528511 (OC)
ISSNs: 2514-8524 (online), 2514-8516 (print)

Contents

	Preface	1
	Definitions	2
	Introduction: Inclusive Publishing and the Quest for Reading Equity	4
1	The Legal and Ethical Context of Inclusive Publishing	17
2	Navigating the Transition to Inclusive Publishing	30
3	Implementing Inclusive Publishing	57
4	Inclusive Publishing beyond Formats	72
	From Book Famine to Reading Equity	89
	References	95

Preface

My journey into inclusive publishing began with a commitment to follow best practice in the ebook production. Throughout my work, I've witnessed both the profound challenges and the extraordinary potential of inclusive publishing. This book represents a culmination of those insights – a bridge between research, advocacy, and practical transformation. Behind every inaccessible book is a story of potential unrealised – of human experiences marginalised, of perspectives unexplored, of research unread. This book seeks to dismantle those invisible barriers, challenging the publishing industry to view accessibility not as a compliance issue, but as a fundamental aspect of creating and sharing stories and knowledge.

This book is based on my research and professional experience with accessibility implementation at Sydney University Press, as well as my involvement with the Australian Inclusive Publishing Initiative (since 2018) and the Round Table on Information Access for People with Print Disabilities Inc. (since 2021). As a member of the Accessibility Initiative Working Party of the Institute of Professional Editors (2020–2023), I co-wrote 'Books without Barriers: A Practical Guide to Inclusive Publishing' (Ganner et al. 2023).

Definitions

This book uses person-first language (i.e. 'person with print disability') and disability-first language ('print-disabled person') interchangeably, in recognition of the diversity of preferences within the disability community. I discuss the two approaches, and the language of disability generally, in Chapter 4.

When using the person-first approach, 'people with print disability' is preferred over 'people with print disabilities' to acknowledge the concept that print disability is a situation or outcome that occurs when the needs of people with certain medical conditions are not met rather than specific impairments. This preference aligns with both the social model and human rights model of disability, which inform other analytical decisions throughout this book. While the social model emphasises disability as a socially constructed barrier, the human rights model further recognises the civil, cultural, economic, political, and social rights of people with disabilities.

Print Disability

George Kerscher of the DAISY Consortium has been commonly credited with creating the term 'print disability'.[1] The data from Google Ngram[2] demonstrates that the term was in use at least by the mid 1970s, and it overtook 'print handicap' by the mid-1980s. The scope of the term 'print disability' has been interpreted differently by various legislative instruments and organisations, but in general it is an umbrella term for a number of temporary or permanent health conditions which can be:

- visual (such as blindness and vision loss; low vision associated with medical conditions such as uncorrected refractive error, age-related macular degeneration, cataract, glaucoma and diabetic retinopathy; and also colour vision deficiency)

---

[1] https://obamawhitehouse.archives.gov/champions/stem-equality-for-americans-with-disabilities/george-kerscher.

[2] https://books.google.com/ngrams/graph?content=print+disability%2Cprint+handicap&year_start=1960&year_end=2019&corpus=en-2019&smoothing=3.

- cognitive and perceptual, affecting sensory processing (such as dyslexia or autistic spectrum disorders), as well as learning difficulties and intellectual disabilities
- physical, including any conditions that make it difficult to manipulate and interact with printed materials (such as arthritis or multiple sclerosis), or to focus or move the eyes (Ganner et al. 2023, 1, 16).

Note

Decisions about who is considered to be 'print disabled' have a significant effect on access to medical and other services, including access to specialist libraries. While such issues are critical in the overall picture, they are outside the scope of this book.

Introduction: Inclusive Publishing and the Quest for Reading Equity

In the context of book publishing, the needs of people with print disability have traditionally been taken care of not by publishers themselves, but by alternative format providers and disability organisations. However, the high cost of accessibility remediation of commercially published books – that is, conversion to formats like audio, large print or braille – has severely limited the number of standard print works that have been converted and made available to people with print disability. While organisations such as the Royal National Institute of Blind People (RNIB) in the UK, or the National Library Service for the Blind and Print Disabled (US Library of Congress) have long existed to provide such support, frequently cited data from the World Blind Union suggests that in 2012 '95% of books in developed countries, and 99% in the least developed world were never converted to accessible formats' (DAISY Consortium n.d.a).[3] This limited access to the written word, broadly referred to as the 'book famine', has affected the opportunities of millions of people to learn, to relax, and to participate in the social, cultural and economic life of society.

Since 2012, the growth of digital technologies has significantly expanded access to books for people with print disability by leveraging the capabilities of assistive technologies and technological advancements in hardware and software. For example, mainstream electronic devices and software increasingly come with built-in accessibility features. Moreover, the affordances of digital reading and the rising popularity of ebooks and audiobooks in mainstream publishing have dramatically widened access to published content beyond accessible formats such as braille, large print, or talking books. Features such as adjustable text size, text-to-speech functionality, and customisable colour contrast now enable individuals with print disability to access mainstream digital content more easily than ever before.

---

[3] Also cited in Rubery 2016, 322. According to Lockyer, Creaser, and Davies (2005) only 4.4 per cent of books published in the UK in 1999–2003 were available in any accessible format.

Inclusive Publishing and the Quest for Reading Equity

Yet, despite the technological advances, as Harpur argues, 'Reading equality remains an unrealised dream that is technologically, commercially, economically and legally possible' (Harpur 2017, 1). There are several reasons for this ongoing inequality, beyond technological and format inaccessibility. Firstly, while technology has been a boon for people with print disability, it can also be a barrier if not designed with accessibility in mind. As Mark Riccobono compellingly argues, 'digital technology is not inherently visual'. Thus, when developers prioritise nonvisual access from the outset, technology can dramatically expand opportunities for individuals with print disability to participate fully in society (Riccobono 2015). Secondly, some books might be 'technologically accessible but not available for use' (Harpur and Stein 2021, 193–94). And, thirdly, some books might be 'technologically accessible but readers lack capacity to consume them' for a variety of reasons, including economic constraints that limit their access to assistive technologies (Harper & Stein 2021, 193–94).

While publishers play a critical role in eliminating both the 'access failure', and the 'market failure', the publishing ecosystem is riddled with systemic challenges including a lack of appropriate tools. Despite technological capabilities, there also remains a pervasive lack of awareness about the reading challenges faced by individuals with print disability. Moreover, the economic incentives for producing fully accessible content remain weak (discussed in Chapter 2), with most publishers treating accessibility as an afterthought rather than a fundamental right.

These systemic challenges to reading inequality are further compounded by insufficient legal mandates. Except for the European Accessibility Act (discussed in Chapter 1), global legal frameworks, although increasingly recognising the rights of people with disabilities, have not mandated publishers to produce content in accessible formats. For example, the Marrakesh Treaty to Facilitate Access to Published Works for Persons Who Are Blind, Visually Impaired or Otherwise Print Disabled (Marrakesh Treaty), the key instrument that removes legal barriers to converting books and other copyright-protected works into accessible formats, perpetuates an exception paradigm where accessible copies are made on an ad hoc basis by the not-for-profit sector. This presents a significant obstacle to reading equality. The intersection of these technological, economic and legal barriers creates a complex ecosystem that perpetuates the 'book famine', making Harpur's depiction of reading equality as an 'unrealised dream' particularly poignant and urgent.

This systemic failure demands a fundamental shift in approach. The current approach to accessibility implementation is trapped in a paradigm of compliance rather than genuine inclusion. We must move beyond legal frameworks that prioritise ad hoc production of accessible formats over actual accessibility implementation; beyond technological solutions that create new barriers while claiming to remove old ones; and beyond publishing models that treat accessible formats as marginal products.

The path forward requires radically reconceptualising how the publishing industry operates. This means moving beyond incremental improvements to a fundamental reimagining of how content is created, distributed, and consumed, and the adoption of truly inclusive publishing workflow. Central to this transformation is placing the experiences of people with print disability at the core of the publishing process, and adopting universal design principles that make accessibility the default, and not the exception, in the writing, editing, design, and production of books. This transition will require developing economic models that support the creation and distribution of accessible content as a core publishing responsibility.

While Paul Harpur argues for reading equality – that is, ensuring that everyone has the same access to reading materials and resources, regardless of their abilities – I propose publishers go a step further and work together with the disability sector towards 'reading equity'. This approach recognises and addresses the diverse needs and challenges that individuals may have in accessing and engaging with materials. Although releasing content that is universally accessible in a single version and format may not be possible, technology now enables the production of multiple, customisable versions and formats tailored to individual needs.

The ultimate barrier to achieving reading equity is not technological or legal, but fundamentally ethical. Reading equity is a human right held in common across languages and countries worldwide, and conventional industry practices remain an impediment to those rights everywhere. Transforming publishing workflows and achieving reading equity requires a multifaceted approach involving cooperation across various sectors, industries, and nations, and a whole-of-publishing-house approach. The transition from ad hoc not-for-profit remediation of accessible formats to commercial production of 'born-accessible' content offers a sustainable and scalable solution to end the book famine. It empowers publishers to meet the growing demand for accessible content and contributes to a more equitable literary landscape where everyone, regardless of ability, has the opportunity to read, learn, and engage with the written word.

While born-accessible reflowable EPUB3 has emerged as a promising universal format, offering unprecedented reader customisation options that serve accessibility needs, we must ensure this emphasis on EPUB doesn't inadvertently marginalise the critical importance of braille access. Braille remains 'a vital tool for literacy, independence, and empowerment' that 'plays a crucial role in the full realization of the human rights and fundamental freedoms of blind and partially sighted people' (WBU 2024). Inclusive publishing must actively consider and support braille reading, whether through traditional embossed materials or digital braille technologies. Indeed, well-structured digital publications can facilitate automated braille transcription, potentially increasing the availability and timeliness of braille materials.

This technological capability to produce customisable formats is beginning to translate into meaningful progress. Even though the book famine is still real, recent advances in accessibility implementation have now gathered a momentum that points towards better access to books for people with print disability in the near future. The European Accessibility Act in particular marks a groundbreaking shift from the not-for-profit conversion of content into accessible formats towards commercial production of born-accessible books by the publishing industry.

As I argue in the book, the shift from conventional publishing to inclusive publishing is transforming the industry. This transformation empowers publishers to remove barriers that have historically excluded people with print disability – not only from accessing books, but also from participating in their creation and production. Rather than presenting inclusive publishing as an aspirational best practice, the evidence reveals a profound industry metamorphosis already underway, exemplified by transformative cases that redefine publishing's core principles.

This book aims to analyse how the transition from conventional to inclusive publishing has fostered progress towards reading equity and transformed how the industry accommodates people with print disability. Through a comprehensive synthesis of this fragmented field, the book examines the broader technological, social, and economic context of this transition towards inclusive publishing, critically assessing policy and regulatory frameworks, publishing initiatives and advocacy efforts to improve access to content for people with print disability and ensure reading equity. While 'inclusive publishing' originates as an advocacy term, not a disciplinary one, critical scholarship can assist the field to develop an agreed common terminology and a clear set of issues, objectives, and practices.

The Difference between 'Accessible' and 'Inclusive' Publishing

Within the publishing industry, the terms 'accessible' and 'inclusive' publishing are often used interchangeably. For example, a number of organisations committed to improving access to published materials by people with print disability include 'inclusive publishing' in their names, such as Inclusive Publishing,[4] Australian Inclusive Publishing Initiative,[5] and Nordic Inclusive Publishing Initiative.[6] At the same time, 'accessible publishing' appears in the names of Publishing Accessibility Action Group (UK),[7] online repositories for information and training resources for the Canadian publishing industry such as Accessible Publishing[8] and Accessible Publishing Learning Network,[9] as well as the DAISY Accessible Publishing Knowledge Base[10] and the Accessible Books Consortium's Charter for Accessible Publishing.[11]

While both terms share the goal of making content available to a wider range of individuals, these approaches reveal critical nuances that can significantly impact how accessibility implementation is understood and enacted.

---

[4] https://inclusivepublishing.org/.   [5] https://aipi.com.au/.
[6] https://nipi.care/.   [7] www.paag.uk.   [8] www.accessiblepublishing.ca/.
[9] https://apln.ca/.   [10] http://kb.daisy.org/publishing/docs/.
[11] www.accessiblebooksconsortium.org/portal/charter.

Accessible publishing

To understand how these approaches differ, it is important to first examine the origins of accessible publishing. Accessible publishing is deeply intertwined with web accessibility standards as defined by the World Wide Web Consortium (W3C) Web Accessibility Initiative (WAI). WAI was established in 1997 to develop 'strategies, standards and resources to help make the Web accessible to people with disabilities' (W3C WAI 2018). The Web Content Accessibility Guidelines (WCAG), first released in 1999, require that information presented digitally should be perceivable, operable, understandable and robust (W3C 2023). Much of the focus of accessible publishing has been on *format* accessibility, technological solutions, and compliance with the standards, which has often resulted in accessibility being treated as a secondary consideration and an afterthought, to be remediated by alternative format producers or implemented at the end of the ebook production stage.

In the world of scholarly and educational publishing, the issue of access also appears in the context of 'open access', a model in which research outputs (journal articles, books or research data) or textbooks (typically referred to as open educational resources) are distributed online, free of cost and other access barriers, typically with a creative commons licence. There are, however, no programmatic requirements for content available in open access to be published in accessible formats or to ensure the writing is accessible. With its focus on removing economic and copyright barriers, open access publishing focuses on the broad and free dissemination of research findings and educational materials, rather than on fostering access to books for people with print disability. Peter Suber acknowledges that other access barriers remain in place, including filtering and censorship, language, 'handicap access', and connectivity barriers (Suber 2012, 13). Writing about library publishing services, Daniel G. Tracy (2015) is one of the rare authors who calls for 'access beyond open', which would consider 'format options, usability, accessibility, and general user experience'.[12]

Within educational publishing, the term 'inclusive access' has been confusingly used to refer to automatic textbook billing – a sales model in

---

[12] See also Carpenter T.A. (2024) and Stack Whitney et al. (2024).

which the cost of digital course content is automatically added to students' tuition and fees.[13] Both open access and 'inclusive access' are outside the scope of this book.

Inclusive Publishing

Inspired by inclusive design principles, inclusive publishing focuses on the production of 'born-accessible' books. The DAISY Consortium (n.d.b.) has defined inclusive publishing as 'the methodology and practice of creating a single, typically commercial publication which can be accessed by everyone irrespective of print disability, using mainstream or specialist assistive technology'.

This recognition of diverse user needs and format-specific considerations aligns with the methodology of inclusive publishing, which builds upon well-established design frameworks used across various industries, such as universal design, inclusive design, user-centred design, accessible design, or design for all, which have been used to achieve a similar goal: 'To provide as effective and usable opportunities as possible for all potential system users, regardless of the challenges, the users may face' (Persson et al. 2015, 524). All these approaches call for a broader range of users to be considered (or take an active part in the design process) to expand the usability of mainstream products and services. Going beyond books and content, Richard Orme, the CEO of the DAISY Consortium, argues for an even broader understanding of inclusive publishing 'to encompass the distribution system, discoverability, accessibility of the library, retail platforms and the reading apps'.[14] This is an essential step to eliminate the various market failures that have created the global book famine.

The term 'inclusive publishing', however, has also been used in the context of supporting diversity, equity, and inclusion in the book publishing industry. According to the *Oxford English Dictionary*, 'The fact or quality of being inclusive' relates in particular to 'the practice or policy of not excluding any person on the grounds of race, gender, religion, age, disability, etc.' The need of the publishing industry to become more diverse

---

[13] www.inclusiveaccess.org/.

[14] Richard Orme, personal communication, 9 December 2021.

and inclusive for staff, authors, and readers has been a topical issue in the UK (Saha & van Lente 2020), the United States (Lee & Bow Books 2016, 2020, 2024), Canada (Association of Canadian Publishers 2019), and Australia (Chowdhury 2020; Driscoll & Bowen 2023) in the past few years. As I argue in this book, accessibility implementation often is and should be part of a broader intersectional approach to diversity and inclusivity. Such an approach is aligned with the human rights model of disability and supports the use of inclusive publishing as a preferred term from the perspective of advocacy.

The Intersection of Disability Models and the Publishing World

The move to inclusive publishing must be understood within the broader context of the development of disability rights in international laws, and the impact of these rights on the lives of people with disability worldwide (discussed in Chapter 1). Specifically, three different disability models (medical, social, and human rights) have been developed over the years, reflecting changing attitudes towards disability and the way society views individuals with impairments.

Traditionally, the publishing industry has operated following the 'medical model' of disability, focusing on the production of books for sighted audiences. In the medical model, the emphasis is on diagnosing the specific impairment or condition (such as visual impairments, dyslexia, or cognitive disorders) that hinder the ability to read and comprehend printed material. The production of alternative formats, such as large print, braille, or audio recordings, has been the purview of disability agencies operating under the exceptions to the national copyright laws. Access to those materials, provided via specialist libraries such as Vision Australia or Bookshare ® or disability services at universities, has been limited to only those with a diagnosis of print disability.

The 'social model' of print disability, a term coined by Mike Oliver in 1981, moves away from 'functional limitations of individuals with impairments' and shifts attention 'onto the problems caused by disabling environments, barriers and cultures' and human rights concerns (Barnes 2020, 20, 26). In this context, print disability 'occurs as a result of the interaction between people living with temporary or permanent health conditions and the barriers to reading they may experience when content is made available in print form only' (Ganner et al. 2023, 1). According to the social model of disability, the barriers to accessing content experienced by people with print disability are created by publishers, software developers, hardware producers, and other stakeholders, who do not take into account their diverse needs and requirements. Overall, the social model emphasises removing barriers and integrating accessibility into mainstream publishing practices, seeing disability as a societal issue.

One of the key criticisms of the social model was the lack of recognition of impairment as a natural aspect of human diversity that governments have a responsibility to support. This led to the development of the 'human rights model' of disability, which is best exemplified by the United Nations Convention on the Rights of Persons with Disabilities (UN CRPD). In comparison to the social model, 'the human rights model is more comprehensive in that it encompasses both sets of human rights, civil and political, as well as economic, social, and cultural rights' (Degener 2017, 44). Article 30 of UN CRPD requires countries that are parties to the convention to ensure 'access to cultural materials', but also to 'take appropriate measures to enable persons with disabilities to have the opportunity to develop and utilize their creative, artistic and intellectual potential, not only for their own benefit, but also for the enrichment of society'. Thus, the human rights model establishes legal frameworks and social expectations that compel publishers towards more inclusive practices – extending beyond mere access to content and encompassing meaningful participation of people with disability in writing and publishing, and in society more broadly (as discussed in Chapter 4). This model reframes accessibility not as voluntary corporate responsibility but as a fundamental legal obligation within an evolving rights-based landscape.

The Emerging Landscape of Research in Inclusive Publishing

Inclusive and/or accessible publishing is a relatively recent area of research and industry practice. The research spans various disciplinary approaches and themes, focusing on the legal and regulatory frameworks, the technology of accessibility, and empirical studies looking at the implementation of accessibility in the publishing industry. As the research landscape reveals, inclusive publishing remains a complex ecosystem of legal, technological, and social challenges that continue to marginalise readers with print disability.

The scholarly discourse spans multiple critical domains, yet has so far failed to translate into meaningful, transformative change. Paul Harpur's seminal work, *Discrimination, Copyright and Equality: Opening the E-book for the Print-disabled* (2017) starkly illustrates this contradiction. For instance, despite the technological opportunities created by digital innovations, existing copyright frameworks continue to negatively impact access to published content. The Marrakesh Treaty, while progressive, has failed to eliminate the book famine, with national and international implementations revealing deep-rooted systemic barriers.[15] The more recent European Accessibility Act has attracted less attention in policy work and scholarly literature thus far,[16] and its impact on the publishing industry is yet to be investigated in detail.

Like the policy landscape, the technological aspect of inclusive publishing faces its own implementation challenges. The technological side is deeply intertwined with web accessibility, and with accessibility in computing and information technologies (ICT) more broadly. The historical trajectory of accessibility research – from the establishment of ACM SIGACCESS in 1971 (Freeman 2022) to contemporary web accessibility studies – demonstrates both progress and persistent limitations. Regrettably, the current picture remains one where the technological potential of accessibility implementation stands in sharp contrast to practical implementation efforts. While researchers have comprehensively mapped web accessibility challenges (Yesilada & Harper 2019), the ICT industry continues to treat accessibility as a peripheral concern rather than a fundamental right.

---

[15] See for example, Fruchterman 2017; Li and Selvadurai 2017; Cassells 2020; Stamm and Hsu 2021; Vleugels 2021; Keller 2023; Helfer 2023 and Ferri 2024.

[16] Ahtonen & Pardo 2013; Drabarz 2020; Ferri 2020; Miller 2024.

The situation within the publishing industry is analogous. For instance, research has consistently identified persistent accessibility issues in PDFs[17] and EPUB files.[18] These technical challenges with file accessibility are symptomatic of issues within the broader publishing ecosystem, as revealed through industry surveys from Australia (Mrva-Montoya 2020a, 2022a), Canada (Association of Canadian Publishers and eBOUND Canada 2020), the European Union (SIDPT 2020), and the UK (Alexander 2022; PAAG 2022), case studies[19] and industry analyses[20] that show a consistent pattern of barriers. Despite growing awareness and numerous best practice guidelines from organisations like the Australian Inclusive Publishing Initiative (AIPI 2019a, 2019b), Accessible Books Consortium,[21] DAISY Consortium,[22] eBOUND Canada (2024), Fondazione LIA (2022), National Network for Equitable Library Service (NNELS),[23] Publishing Accessibility Action Group,[24] and others,[25] the implementation of accessibility remains inconsistent and inadequate.

Notwithstanding these persistent barriers to implementation, emerging research offers glimpses of potential transformation. For example, innovative approaches such as using computer algorithms for book recommendation systems for visually impaired readers suggest the possibility of technological solutions (Yu et al. 2020). The published case studies and industry analyses mentioned earlier – from collaborative approaches to

---

[17] For example, Acosta-Vargas et al. 2020; Fayyaz et al. 2021; Darvishy et al. 2023; Kumar and Wang 2024 and Szentirmai et al. 2024.

[18] For example, Schwarz et al. 2018; Suzuki & Yamaguchi 2020 and Taylor 2021.

[19] Conrad & Kasdorf 2018; Kasdorf 2018; see also Abbott 2018; Scott 2022; Cooper et al. 2023; Rosenberg et al. 2023; Wells Ajinkya et al. 2023.

[20] Axelrod 2018; Bowes III 2018; House et al. 2018; Iglesias 2018; McNaught et al. 2018; Turner 2018.

[21] Gunn 2016. See also www.accessiblebooksconsortium.org.

[22] Hilderley 2013 [2011]. See also https://daisy.org/; https://inclusivepublishing.org/, https://kb.daisy.org/publishing/docs/.

[23] www.accessiblepublishing.ca. [24] www.paag.uk/paag-resources/.

[25] Garrish 2012; Rosen 2018; BISG 2019; Ganner et el. 2023; Round Table 2024. See also the Canadian Accessible Publishing Learning Network, https://apln.ca/.

image accessibility to the implementation of plain language summaries – provide roadmaps for incremental progress.

Yet even as these solutions emerge, the research landscape itself reflects the marginalisation it seeks to address. Indeed, as Forget and Wingate's recent bibliography (2024) pointedly demonstrates, the intersection of book history and disability studies remains remarkably under-researched – a scholarly silence that is itself a form of exclusion.

About the Book

This book is based on a review of the published literature and empirical studies. It focuses on developments in Australia, Canada, the European Union, the UK, and the United States. The digital revolution has radically transformed the publishing landscape, expanding both who can publish and what constitutes publishing through social media and digital platforms. Nevertheless, *Inclusive Publishing and the Quest for Reading Equity* centres on traditional book publishers – those producing long-form writing in print, digital, and audio formats across commercial/trade, educational, and scholarly sectors.

These publishing sectors operate under distinct dynamics, and despite ongoing industry consolidation and globalisation, they maintain a remarkable plurality of voices and diversity of ownership. An organisation's sector and size significantly influence its capacity and approach to implementing accessibility measures: from multinational publishers with dedicated accessibility teams to independent presses with limited resources. Yet, the fundamental principles of inclusive publishing transcend these organisational boundaries. Although this book primarily examines traditional book publishing, its insights are equally valuable for self-publishing ventures and non-book content creators, who face similar challenges in making their content accessible to all readers.

Chapter 1 provides a broader context to accessibility implementation by discussing the legal and social forces that have shaped the 'accessibility turn' in the publishing industry, such as the Universal Declaration of Human Rights; the Marrakesh Treaty to Facilitate Access to Published Works for Persons Who Are Blind, Visually Impaired, or Otherwise Print Disabled

(Marrakesh Treaty); and the European Accessibility Act (EAA). As argued earlier, the EAA constitutes a paradigm shift by requiring publishers to fund and produce accessible formats of books, and its impact extends beyond the European Union.

Chapter 2 examines the main concerns and challenges related to accessibility implementation, as well as strategic advantages for publishers who adopt inclusive publishing workflows. While government regulation and public policy have a role to play in the transition to inclusive publishing, I argue that strategic partnerships and collaborations with the disability sector and other organisations are essential to drive the industry transformation.

In Chapter 3, I discuss the key elements of inclusive publishing at an organisational level. This includes the importance of having accessibility principles embedded in policy, workflows, and quality assurance processes in order to produce born-accessible publications. Inclusive publishing encompasses the entire publishing ecosystem and book supply chain. It is proactive, comprehensive, and more cost-effective and efficient than remediating content at the end of the publishing process to comply with the legal mandates and accessibility standards.

Chapter 4 expands the focus beyond accessible formats to look at three areas where disability and publishing studies intersect: the paucity of staff with disability working in publishing, the lack of representation of people with disability in books, and the question of inclusive and accessible language. Using an intersectional lens, I argue that inclusive publishing needs to go beyond accessible content and formats. Creating born-accessible publications should go together with making the publishing industry inclusive of people with print and other disabilities, as staff, authors, and characters in the books, while acknowledging that disability is intertwined with other aspects of identity and marginalisation.

Finally, the book concludes by surveying key trends in inclusive publishing and identifying critical areas for future research. The conclusion serves as a call for publishers, content creators, and other industry stakeholders to adopt a proactive, inclusive mindset, recognising that true inclusivity goes beyond removing barriers to access.

1 The Legal and Ethical Context of Inclusive Publishing

National copyright laws, originating with the 1886 Berne Convention for the Protection of Literary and Artistic Works initially focused on protecting creators' economic and moral rights. These copyright frameworks inadvertently erected significant barriers for individuals with print disability, by granting creators exclusive rights to control the use and distribution of their works that effectively prevented the reproduction and distribution of works in accessible formats without explicit permission. This exclusionary legal structure effectively created a book famine that marginalised individuals with visual impairments or other print-related disabilities, essentially creating a form of systemic information discrimination.

The evolution of copyright exceptions for accessibility reflects a profound conceptual transformation in how society understands disability itself. Early copyright modifications emerged from charitable and medical models that viewed print disability as an individual deficit requiring special accommodation. Over the years, the provision of books to the print disabled has been facilitated by a progressive evolution of national copyright laws that increasingly recognise information access as the fundamental human right rather than charitable concession. This legislative transformation mirrors the broader paradigm shift from medical and social models towards a human rights approach to disability – one that frames accessibility not as accommodation but as an essential legal obligation necessary for full societal participation and equal dignity. These copyright reforms embody the principles enshrined in the United Nations Convention on the Rights of Persons with Disabilities, acknowledging that barriers to information access constitute discrimination requiring systematic legal remedy.

The United States provides a compelling case study in the gradual expansion of accessibility rights. The Pratt-Smoot Act adopted on 3 March 1931 represented one of the first legislative efforts to address the information needs of blind individuals. By authorising the provision of books in braille for blind adult readers and establishing a free national library programme administered by the National Library Service (NLS), the act acknowledged that access to information is a critical component of social participation and it represented a clear application of the social model of disability. By creating infrastructure for braille books and a dedicated library service, the act addressed the environmental and institutional barriers that create disability. The 1933 amendment to include talking books further demonstrated a growing understanding of diverse accessibility needs and evolving technology. While the act was transformational, the NLS needed to first secure permission from the rights holders before converting a copyrighted work into alternative formats, which caused delays.

This changed in 1996, when the Chafee Amendment was passed. It created an exception and limitation to copyright law that allows authorised entities to transcribe materials for persons with print disability. This amendment removed the need to obtain permission from the copyright holders, expanded the audience for special formats beyond individuals with no vision, and facilitated more rapid and efficient production of accessible formats.

Apart from the Chafee Amendment, the fair use doctrine also provides a provision for 'the making of copies or phonorecords of works in the special forms needed for the use of blind persons' without the need to get the copyright owner's permission.[26] This dual approach – specific amendments and broader fair use provisions – created a more robust legal framework for information accessibility.

In April 2024, the US Department of Justice finalised a landmark rule under Title II of the Americans with Disabilities Act (ADA) requiring state and local governments to make their websites and mobile applications fully accessible to people with disabilities. This comprehensive regulation impacts all state and local government entities, including public educational institutions from K–12 schools to universities and public libraries, mandating that their digital content meets specific accessibility standards. While publishers are not directly regulated by this rule, they face significant

---

[26] 17 U.S.C. United States Code, 2010 Edition Title 17 – Copyrights Chapter 1 – Subject Matter and Scope of Copyright Sec. 107 – Limitations on exclusive rights: Fair use from the US Government Publishing Office, www.govinfo.gov/content/pkg/USCODE-2010-title17/html/USCODE-2010-title17-chap1-sec107.htm.

indirect implications as government agencies increasingly demand ADA-compliant educational materials and digital content to satisfy their own legal obligations.[27]

The US example demonstrates how exception laws evolved: expanding the focus from people who are blind to those with print disability more broadly, incorporating formats beyond braille, and eliminating the need for publisher permission. This broadening scope reflects a global shift, as international human rights instruments prompted nations worldwide to re-examine their copyright laws through the lens of disability rights and social inclusion. With the exception of the European Accessibility Act; however, they stop short of requiring publishers to produce accessible formats.

In this chapter, I focus on these international legal and social forces that have shaped the recent 'accessibility turn' in publishing, using Gian Maria Greco's term. Greco's powerful observation that '[T]he accessibility revolution has been pervading and radically changing the very foundation of our society, bringing access to the fore as a crucial issue in our age' (Greco 2018, 206) captures the transformative potential of this paradigm shift. Its genesis is closely connected with the cultural and societal revolution created by the Universal Declaration of Human Rights (UDHR), the adoption of the United Nations Convention on the Rights of Persons with Disabilities (UN CRPD), and the impact of these international human rights instruments on national legislative, administrative, and judicial practices around the world. In the context of the publishing industry, the Marrakesh Treaty to Facilitate Access to Published Works for Persons who are Blind, Visually Impaired or Otherwise Print Disabled (Marrakesh Treaty), and the European Accessibility Act (EAA) are of particular salience. While the Marrakesh Treaty relies on non-for-profits and specialised libraries to provide access to books, the EAA directly influences the market by requiring publishers to invest in making their products and services accessible for the European market.

---

[27] Americans with Disabilities Act Title II Regulations, www.ada.gov/law-and-regs/regulations/title-ii-2010-regulations/. 'ADA Title II: How Does the New Ruling Affect You?' *Inclusive Publishing*, 17 November 2024. https://inclusivepublishing.org/blog/ada-title-ii-how-does-the-new-ruling-affect-you/.

International Human Rights Instruments

International human rights instruments have progressively transformed our understanding of human dignity and equality. The UDHR proclaimed by the United Nations General Assembly in Paris on 10 December 1948 emerged as a groundbreaking document that recognised that 'the inherent dignity of all members of the human family is the foundation of freedom, justice and peace in the world'. Beyond its philosophical significance, UDHR comprehensively articulated civil and political rights (such as the right to life, liberty, security, free speech, and privacy), and economic, social, and cultural rights (such as the right to health, work, education, and social security), forming the basis of international human rights law and more than seventy human rights treaties, including the UN CRPD.

According to Paul Harpur, the UN CRPD, which was adopted in 2006 and entered into force 3 May 2008, complemented the original declaration and ushered in a new rights-based disability model that had a profound impact on legal frameworks and global discourse around digital reading equality. The treaty framed having access to accessible information and communication technologies as a fundamental human right for persons with disability. Its innovative framework requires its signatories to implement a comprehensive disability-rights-based agenda that extends far beyond legal reforms. The UN CRPD mandates states to raise awareness, combat stereotypes and prejudices, and promote the capabilities and contributions of persons with disabilities (Harpur 2017, 32–33, 44–45), while also requiring to 'take all appropriate steps to ensure that reasonable accommodation is provided' when implementing measures 'to promote equality and eliminate discrimination' (Art. 5(3)). This rights-centred approach acknowledges that accessibility is not optional but a necessary condition for persons with disabilities to fully participate in society and enjoy their human rights on an equal basis with others.

Critically, the UN CRPD provisions directly address information access, compelling states to ensure persons with disabilities can 'enjoy access to cultural materials in accessible formats' (Art. 30). The states are also required to '[urge] private entities' and '[encourage] mass media' to 'provide information and services in accessible and usable formats for persons with disabilities'

(Art. 21(c) and (d)), thereby transforming accessibility from an optional consideration to a fundamental social responsibility.

The UN CRPD directly addresses reading equity by mandating that state parties ensure intellectual property rights do not create unreasonable or discriminatory barriers to cultural materials access for persons with disabilities (Art. 30(3)). The convention further compels states to 'undertake or promote research and development of universally designed goods, services, equipment and facilities ... which should require the minimum possible adaptation and the least cost to meet the specific needs of a person with disabilities, to promote their availability and use' (Art. 2).

The UN CRPD provides a comprehensive definition of universal design as 'the design of products, environments, programmes and services to be usable by all people, to the greatest extent possible, without the need for adaptation or specialized design'. Crucially, while emphasising universal design, the convention explicitly ensures that assistive devices for specific groups of persons remain essential (Art. 2), calling for reading equity rather than just equality. In the publishing context, born-accessible digital books like reflowable EPUB3 files most effectively embody the criteria of inclusively designed products. However, ensuring the ongoing production of traditional accessible formats such as braille books, which are specifically mentioned in the UN CRPD, remains crucial for reading equity.

The convention's transformative impact extends far beyond theoretical frameworks. It has directly influenced international copyright laws, catalysing the adoption of the Marrakesh Treaty (Harpur 2017, 65), and the EAA. Moreover, the UN CRPD compels signatory states to align their domestic legislation, policies, and practices with the obligations contained in the convention, ensuring a systematic approach to accessibility and disability rights.

The Marrakesh Treaty

As international human rights frameworks evolved to prioritise accessibility, the Marrakesh Treaty emerged as a crucial mechanism for transforming these principles into actionable copyright law. Adopted by member states of the World Intellectual Property Organization (WIPO) on 28 June 2013 and entering into force on 30 September 2016, the treaty represents a pivotal breakthrough in improving access to books for persons with print disability. The treaty mandates that signatories incorporate minimum baseline copyright provisions which enable people with print disability (or organisations acting on their behalf) to create and share accessible formats of copyrighted works, while also facilitating a cross-border exchange of accessible copies produced according to the limitations and exceptions it provides.

In Australia, for example, the treaty's implementation led to a comprehensive legislative transformation. The Copyright Amendment (Disability Access and Other Measures) Act 2017 fundamentally redesigned disability access provisions by removing references to specific impairments. Instead, the law now defines 'a person with a disability' as 'an individual who has difficulty reading, viewing, hearing or comprehending copyright material in a particular form'. This approach creates a more inclusive framework that encompasses all disabilities, all types of materials, and all required formats. The amendment replaced the previous narrow exception with a fair dealing exception, and also replaced statutory licences with 'a single exception that applies to organisations assisting persons with a disability'. Critically, it defines 'organisation assisting persons with a disability' as 'educational institutions and not-for-profit organisations with a principal function of providing assistance to persons with a disability', permitting them to produce and distribute accessible format copies when such materials are not commercially available within a reasonable timeframe and at standard commercial pricing.

Despite its groundbreaking nature, the Marrakesh Treaty has significant limitations in eliminating reading inequity. As Stamm and Hsu critically observe, the treaty does not compel countries to develop inclusive policies for people with disabilities, and crucially, 'Publishers are not affected by the Marrakesh Treaty and are allowed to continue producing their books in inaccessible formats' (Stamm & Hsu 2021, 692). In other words, the treaty focuses primarily on the provision of specialist formats and *not* the promotion of born-accessible mainstream content, effectively maintaining a marginal approach to disability access.

The treaty's structural approach perpetuates what Harpur describes as an 'exception paradigm' that merely tolerates limited unauthorised dealings

(Harpur 2017, 75). By relying on public and non-profit organisations to be 'the main facilitators of access to useable content by vision-impaired people' (Adair & Harpur 2019, 400), it permits the creation of accessible copies on an ad hoc basis, allowing individuals with disabilities to access individual titles through authorised institutions using adaptive technologies. This model inherently constrains access as 'the creation of accessible copies is still costly and slow, obtaining access remains the exception, rather than the norm' (Harpur 2017, 75).

Nonetheless, the treaty has made meaningful strides in expanding book access for people with print disability. Even though Harpur argues that 'the tolerance model to disability access is not providing adequate access', and 'fall[s] short of human rights obligations in the CRPD', he acknowledges that the treaty has expanded access to books for people with print disability (Harpur 2017, 77, 81–83). Practical implementations demonstrate this potential. For example, Bookshare ®, an online library of accessible books originally limited to audiences in the United States, now operates internationally through partnerships with various libraries and organisations for the blind.[28] Similarly, the ABC Global Book Service of the Accessible Books Consortium, a public–private partnership launched in June 2014 by the World Intellectual Property Organization and a group of key partners to support the Marrakesh Treaty on a practical level, provides a global platform for accessible digital books.

Apart from facilitating access to existing libraries of accessible content, the Marrakesh Treaty has also stimulated broader accessibility conversations within the publishing industry worldwide. By creating an international framework for accessible content exchange, it has highlighted the critical importance of inclusive publishing practices and sparked implementation efforts across several countries, as explored in Chapter 2.

The European Accessibility Act

Following the progressive international developments in disability rights, the European Accessibility Act (EAA) emerges as a landmark legislative instrument aimed at standardising and mainstreaming accessibility across

[28] www.bookshare.org/.

physical environments, transport, and information and communication technologies. Described as 'the most ambitious of the EU legislative steps towards accessibility' (Drabarz 2020, 85–86), the EAA distinguishes itself from previous instruments by directly addressing accessibility of mainstream content in the publishing sector.

The act's development traces a deliberate path of international commitment. After the European Union (EU) ratified UN CRPD in January 2011, organisations and government entities in its member states have been bound to fulfil the obligations of the convention. By 2014, the EU had adopted several legal acts to harmonise accessibility requirements for goods and services (Drabarz 2020, 83–85). The EU's strategic approach continued with the signing of the Marrakesh Treaty on 30 April 2014, and the creation of implementing directive on 13 September 2017.[29] Building on these legal instruments, the EU adopted the EAA in 2019, with implementation mandated for EU member states by 28 June 2022, and full enforcement set for 28 June 2025.

The directive's scope is comprehensive, aiming to improve the EU internal market's functioning by removing barriers created by divergent accessibility regulations in member states. Businesses in the EU stand to gain from streamlined accessibility regulations facilitating cost reduction, simplified cross-border trading, and expanded 'market opportunities for their accessible products and services'. Individuals with disability and elderly people are expected to experience improved accessibility through the availability of more competitive and affordable products and services, reduced barriers in transportation, education, and the job market, and increased job opportunities for people with accessibility expertise. Notably, in the context of publishing, the EAA's coverage extends to a diverse range of products and services, including ebooks, ereaders, and ecommerce platforms, signalling a holistic approach to accessibility in the book ecosystem.

---

[29] Directive (EU) 2017/1564 of the European Parliament and of the Council of 13 September 2017 on certain permitted uses of certain works and other subject matter protected by copyright and related rights for the benefit of persons who are blind, visually impaired or otherwise print-disabled and amending Directive 2001/29/EC on the harmonisation of certain aspects of copyright and related rights in the information society; also the Regulation (EU) 2017/1563.

Most importantly, in contrast to the exception-based Marrakesh Treaty, the EAA requires publishers to produce their digital publications in accessible and interoperable formats, which 'should optimise the compatibility of those files with the user agents and with current and future assistive technologies'. Following the UN CRPD, the EAA recommends a universal design or 'design for all' approach to the creation of products and services (41, 50). In essence, the EAA requires publishers to operate from the social model of disability; that is, to remove barriers to content access for people with print disability by publishing born-accessible digital books.

The legislation's approach is notably flexible, avoiding detailed technical restrictions to allow for innovation while referencing the Web Content Accessibility Guidelines (WCAG) and requiring accessibility metadata (Annex I, Section IV(f)). Moreover, the EAA emphasises collaborative implementation, directly stipulating the need for cooperation between authorities and relevant stakeholders, including persons with disability and disability organisations, to improve coherence and monitor the implementation of the provisions of EAA (96). This comprehensive approach extends beyond publishers to the entire supply chain, which will need to make content available to users through accessible services.

Recognising practical constraints, the EAA includes nuanced provisions for smaller businesses. Microenterprises – that is, businesses with fewer than 10 employees and an annual turnover or a balance sheet total of no more than €2 million (EU, n.d.) – are exempt from the obligations of the act, though encouraged to comply. Moreover, member states are required to 'provide guidelines and tools to microenterprises to facilitate the application of national measures transposing this Directive'. Additionally, companies may seek an exemption by demonstrating 'evidence of the disproportionate burden or fundamental alteration' (68) – which, as Laura Brady observes, could particularly impact 'highly visual content like comics and graphic novels, children's books, and art books' (Brady 2024). While exemptions to the EAA may provide short-term relief to publishers, they could also lead to long-term challenges in accessibility implementation and impede overall progress towards a more inclusive publishing environment.

The EAA's effectiveness in addressing the reading equity remains uncertain, despite its ambitious goals. Jeffrey Archer Miller critically observes that the European Commission's strategic framing of the EAA as a 'business-friendly venture rather than an anti-discrimination initiative' potentially undermines its comprehensive implementation (Miller 2024, 190). The EAA rollout has been plagued by significant implementation challenges. Sixteen out of twenty-seven EU member states missed the June 2022 deadline for taking measures to transpose the EAA into their national laws (European Union of the Deaf 2022) and by February 2024, Bulgaria, Cyprus, the Netherlands, and Poland had yet to do so (Brady 2024). This delayed implementation raises serious questions about the act's practical impact.

The publishing landscape further complicates the EAA's implementation. The industry is predominantly composed of microenterprises that fall outside the act's scope. The publishing ecosystem in Poland, for example, illustrates this complexity: in 2023 there were only forty large publishers with an annual income of over €5 million. Meanwhile, there were 206 medium-sized publishers with an annual income of €215,000 to €5 million, over 1,600 small publishers with an annual income of less than €200,000 and publishing at least two titles a year, and over 4,000 irregular publishers producing an occasional publication (Polish Book Institute 2023). While large publishers have the potential to make significant strides in widening access to books through their extensive publishing programmes and the sheer scale of their operations, smaller, independent presses are crucial to maintaining bibliodiversity (Hawthorne 2014). Encouragingly, some smaller presses are already demonstrating leadership in proactively embracing inclusive publishing practices, for example, Hegas in Sweden.

The June 2025 implementation date presents a critical challenge, particularly for the backlist titles. There are legitimate concerns that many existing publications may disappear from the market if they are not remediated in time. Recognising these difficulties, some countries have adopted more flexible approaches. France and Italy, for instance, have instituted a five-year transition period until 2030, leveraging Article 32 of the EAA to provide publishers with additional time to implement accessibility measures in their backlist titles (Brady 2024).

The enforcement mechanism of the EAA operates through a decentralised framework, with each EU member state wielding significant discretion in implementing and enforcing compliance measures. While the act mandates that enforcement measures must be 'effective, proportionate, and dissuasive', and 'take into account the extent of the non-compliance' (Art. 30), this flexibility has led to varying approaches across jurisdictions. The established penalty structure imposes fines ranging from €5,000 to €7,500 per infraction, encompassing a broad spectrum of accessibility violations: from inaccessible content and problematic digital rights management implementation to inadequate reading system accessibility, missing accessibility metadata, and inaccessible purchasing experiences. Significantly, the enforcement mechanism empowers both individual consumers and disability organisations to report compliance issues, creating a collaborative monitoring system (Brady 2024).

This nuanced and multi-stakeholder approach suggests a recognition of the complex challenges facing publishers while maintaining a commitment to increasing accessibility. However, the ultimate success of the EAA will depend on continued momentum, supportive policy frameworks, and a genuine commitment to inclusive publishing across the European publishing ecosystem.

While the EAA is of particular salience to European publishers, it will affect any organisation wanting to sell ebooks in the European market, so its influence will be much greater. Moreover, as multinational publishers implement inclusive publishing practices to produce EAA-compliant books, they are likely to introduce these practices to their operations in other territories. The rest of the publishing world will also benefit from the knowledge and experience of European publishers in tackling accessibility implementation. The potential for the EAA to have a global impact is consistent with the 'Brussels effect'; that is, 'the EU's unilateral power to regulate global markets'. As Anu Bradford argues, 'The EU today promulgates regulations that influence which products are built and how business is conducted, not just in Europe but everywhere in the world' (Bradford 2020, xv).

The regulatory power of legislation like the EAA becomes especially crucial given that, according to Paul Harpur, corporate social responsibility, soft law, and self-regulation 'cannot be relied upon to motivate corporations to promote digital equality' (2017, 28), particularly in a setting where there are conflicting interests vying for publishers' attention, such as diversity, equity and inclusion, or sustainability issues.

Legal imperatives such as the EAA play a significant role in galvanising the industry's move towards inclusive publishing practices. Even if publishers outside the EU are not directly affected by national legal instruments, they may still need to comply indirectly with various public procurement requirements. For example, in Australia, following the ratification of the Marrakesh Treaty in 2016, the national (government) procurement rules were revised, requiring not only all levels of government but also public libraries and educational institutions to procure digital products, services, and content that meet accessibility requirements (Standards Australia 2016; AIPI 2019a, 13). In the United States, there has been 'a series of legal cases against universities providing inaccessible materials to students' (Trimble 2018, 21; see also Iglesias 2018, 50). As mentioned before, in the current US legal framework, which includes the Americans with Disabilities Act (1990) and other relevant legislature including Section 504 of the Rehabilitation Act of 1973, it is the schools and universities that are liable, not the publishers. However, this situation is impacting educational publishing houses too, because some universities and their libraries have started including accessibility requirements in their procurement policies (Wood et al. 2017, 29; Axelrod 2018, 42). Those major educational publishers that are moving towards the production of accessible content are gaining competitive advantage over those that are not. These companies are then rolling out accessibility implementation across their subsidiaries in other countries too, so the impact of the legal cases against educational institutions in the United States is far reaching.

This cascade of regulatory and market pressures across different jurisdictions demonstrates how accessibility requirements are becoming increasingly embedded in the global publishing ecosystem. And the implications extend far beyond publishing. By challenging existing paradigms of production and distribution, these legal and social forces are reshaping our understanding of design, technology, and social participation. They represent a profound recognition that disability is not a deviation from a norm, but a fundamental characteristic of human experience.

Greco's concept of the 'accessibility revolution' is thus more than a metaphor. It represents a fundamental reimagining of social structures, challenging us to create systems that are inherently inclusive rather than retrofitting accessibility as an afterthought. The publishing industry becomes a microcosm of this larger societal transformation – an arena where legal innovation, technological capability, and human rights discourse converge to create more equitable modes of knowledge dissemination. The progress towards inclusive publishing varies significantly between nations and industry sectors due to a complex interplay of factors: a combination of regulatory requirements, market demands, advocacy efforts, and leadership within publishing organisations.

This chapter has traced how international human rights instruments, copyright reforms, and accessibility legislation have progressively transformed the publishing landscape, moving from an exception-based model that relied on specialised formats to a rights-based framework that demands mainstream accessible publishing. While these legal and regulatory developments, particularly the EAA, create powerful incentives for change, they alone cannot guarantee successful implementation of inclusive publishing practices. As the industry navigates this complex regulatory landscape and grapples with implementation challenges, the next chapter examines how some publishers have developed effective accessibility strategies through collaborative partnerships with disability organisations, arguing that such alliances are essential for driving meaningful transformation beyond mere compliance.

2 Navigating the Transition to Inclusive Publishing

Publishers play a critical role in eliminating 'access failure' and enabling access to copyright material for individuals with print disability. As early as 2004, George Kerscher and Jennifer Sutton of the DAISY Consortium argued that publishers' commitment to 'making their works fully accessible to persons with print disabilities . . . should be a corporate business decision that becomes fundamental to a publishing house' based on clear social, legal, and business imperatives (Kerscher & Sutton 2004). In 2005, Frederick Bowes III called on 'publishers to develop and implement informed operating policies and protocols that assure that on an ongoing basis its products and services meet applicable accessibility requirements and thus can fully compete in an increasingly demanding marketplace' (Bowes III 2005, 45). Although these imperatives are clear, implementing accessibility considerations in the publishing workflows has proven challenging.

As discussed in the previous chapter, the adoption of the EAA is set to be a game changer on a global scale from mid 2025. Changes in the legal frameworks that focus on disability rights, however, do not automatically translate into meaningful systemic transformation. In fact, the 2004 US National Council of Disability report, *Design for Inclusion: Creating a New Marketplace*, identified legislation as both a facilitator and a barrier to universal design. Government accessibility mandates create powerful market forces, as manufacturers cannot ignore standards backed by regulatory requirements and substantial public purchasing power. However, these same regulations often undermine accessibility through conflicting jurisdictional requirements, outdated frameworks that lag behind technological innovation, vague guidelines leading to inconsistent interpretations, inadequate enforcement allowing false accessibility claims, and solutions that fail to reach users of older technology (National Council on Disability 2004).

Moreover, as Goggin and Newell point out, the media has been slow to implement accessibility, due to the 'industry's either outright opposition, passive ignorance, acts of omission, or unwillingness to embrace required change' (Goggin & Newell 2007, 161). In many areas, progress has relied on the work of not-for-profits and industry-based organisations as part of 'self-regulation' efforts, a policymaking strategy which has been common since at least 1995, with a poor record of success. Consequently, Goggin and Newell call for 'co-regulation', combining a market-driven approach and self-regulation, where 'standards-setting bodies, regulatory agencies, and governments' provide strong models (Goggin & Newell 2007, 164–66). This multifaceted approach is now unfolding within the publishing industry. A number of global and national initiatives, and a growing recognition of the importance of inclusive publishing, have provided the publishing industry around the world with the impetus to improve access to publications for people with print disability.

In this chapter I examine the critical barriers impeding accessibility implementation – from technical complexity and resource constraints to organisational resistance and knowledge gaps. This analysis serves as an essential context for understanding the subsequent exploration of influential global organisations, strategic partnerships, and industry self-regulation initiatives that have been instrumental in raising awareness, and the development of guidelines and training. I argue that collaborations and strategic partnerships have been and will continue to be essential in assisting the publishing industry to manage the transition to commercial production of born-accessible books and improving access to information for people with print disability. This chapter moves beyond examining the initial 'accessibility turn' in publishing to specifically investigating how the industry is progressing towards a model of inclusive publishing – a holistic approach where accessibility is integrated into standard workflows rather than treated as an accommodation or afterthought. By analysing this evolution, we can better understand how collaborative efforts are reshaping publishing practices to ensure reading equity and universal access by design.

The Barriers to Inclusion: Key Concerns and Challenges

These collaborative efforts emerge in response to significant obstacles facing publishers across international markets, as evidenced by recent industry research. The findings of industry surveys in Australia (Mrva-Montoya 2020a, 2022a), Canada (Association of Canadian Publishers and eBOUND Canada 2020), the European Union (SIDPT 2020), and the UK (Alexander 2022; PAAG 2022) show similar barriers to the production, distribution, and discovery of accessible books in various markets. These include limited knowledge; a lack of capacity, including staffing resources; the cost of implementation; and concerns around copyright.

Accessibility and Print Disability Knowledge

The landscape of accessibility knowledge is inherently complex, compounded by limited understanding of print disability. Existing accessibility guidelines tend to focus on the technical and conformance aspects of the formats, presenting significant challenges for publishers. The web and EPUB accessibility standards are written in a highly technical language that can be difficult for publishing professionals to interpret and implement effectively.

Moreover, with their expertise focused on producing print materials for the mainstream audience, publishing professionals often lack comprehensive understanding of the specific formats required for readers with print disability and how these individuals interact with different formats. The diversity of reading needs among people with print disability is profound, with requirements that can vary significantly and sometimes contradict each other depending on the type(s) of disability. For example, the accessibility needs of readers who are blind differ substantially from those who have low vision or other forms of visual disability (such as colour blindness) or learning disabilities and cognitive impairments. This complexity presents significant challenges in design and production. Graphic designers, in particular, rarely consider the needs of people with print disability, be it visual, physical or cognitive as noted by Hendel (2013, 31–33) and in Huang's (2023) work on colour vision deficiency.

Moreover, the lack of knowledge of print disability can be partly explained by the paucity of publishing staff with lived experience of disability, and a shortage of books written by disabled authors and that represent disabled characters, as discussed in Chapter 4, so people are unable to read about diverse experiences. This dual lack of representation is a problem the industry must continue to proactively address via hiring policies and acquisition strategies.

To complicate the issue further, according to Laura Brady, people who do become accessibility experts or advocates find they can earn much better salaries in other industries. The brain drain from trade publishing in Canada, for example, has been significant.[30]

Policy, Capacity, and Cost Concerns

At the organisational level, many publishers lack formal policy or accessibility strategies that would underpin accessibility implementation. This challenge is compounded by significant concerns about the capacity, staffing resources, and costs associated with the production and distribution of accessible publications. For example, 40 per cent of educational publishers self-reported concerns about 'the amount of work and financial cost involved' in a 2022 survey (Mrva-Montoya 2022a, 741). These concerns affect three areas: the implementation of inclusive publishing workflows, the production of born-accessible books, and the conversion of backlist and legacy content. It is clear that treating accessibility as an afterthought is expensive. However, the adoption of inclusive publishing practices also requires staffing and financial resources, to train staff, develop policy and briefs, change workflows, and potentially invest in certification.

The production cost of born-accessible books depends on the genre of content, its complexity, the publisher's workflow, and the tools used. Publishers typically have no control over the software or hardware used to create or access content. Adobe InDesign remains the predominant software in the publishing industry, with compelling statistical evidence underscoring its ubiquity: a 2020 Australian survey of publishers revealed that 85 per cent of those who produced ebooks in-house used this platform (Mrva-Montoya 2020a, 15), while a 2022 UK survey found 58 per cent of publishers continuing to use it (Alexander 2022, 700; PAAG 2022). However, this widespread reliance presents a critical paradox: despite the status of Adobe InDesign as an industry standard tool, the software has historically struggled to fully support the production of accessible EPUB3 files upon export. While recent months have witnessed incremental improvements, the persistent technological limitations underscore a significant barrier to comprehensive digital accessibility in publishing.

---

[30] Laura Brady, personal communication, 21 February 2024.

Even when accessibility technical specifications are embedded in the digital workflow and automated, publishers need to allocate additional resources to produce good-quality alternative text (and, if needed, long text descriptions) for images, tables, and other multimedia. The costs can be significant, particularly in publications with complex content and layouts (such as textbooks and educational media, highly illustrated books, and STEM publications). Empirical evidence underscores the severity of this challenge: a 2022 UK survey revealed that 77 per cent of publishers identified the provision of meaningful alt text as their primary accessibility obstacle, with a staggering 55 per cent of respondents reporting including image descriptions in less than 10 per cent of their content (Alexander 2022, 700). The magnitude of this issue becomes even more apparent in scholarly publishing, where a comprehensive analysis of nearly 20,000 scholarly PDFs published between 2014 and 2023 found that only 8.5 per cent contained alt text. This systemic deficit prompted Kumar and Wang (2024) to advocate for a comprehensive, multi-dimensional strategy – calling for sophisticated technological development, comprehensive author education, and fundamental restructuring of academic publishing practices to address this critical accessibility gap.

The conversion of backlist titles represents another formidable economic and technical challenge for publishers, particularly in Europe, where the EAA imposes a critical compliance deadline of June 2025. The Accessible Backlist Ebooks Laboratory (ABELab) project,[31] strategically funded by the EU Creative Europe programme, has emerged as a key initiative to identify key issues and develop comprehensive guidelines for publishers on cost-effective remediation of their backlists. Their preliminary analysis reveals that more than 3.5 million ebook titles were available in different digital formats via European ecommerce platforms in early 2023. This number excludes international platforms such as Amazon, Apple, Google, and Kobo, so the actual number is much higher.

The heterogeneity of digital formatting presents a particularly nuanced challenge. An in-depth examination of five EU countries exposes significant

---

[31] www.abelab.eu/.

disparities in ebook formats: Germany's backlist is predominantly PDF-based, with 60 per cent of files available in this format and only 3 per cent available as EPUB3 files. In contrast, France and Italy demonstrate a markedly different profile with nearly 40 per cent of backlist titles in EPUB3 format and less than 25 per cent in PDF. The remediation efforts required to make these formats accessible, as well as different genres of books, is expected to vary significantly; publications with complex layouts in PDF will require the most work.

Moreover, the historical context of digital publishing compounds these challenges. EPUB3 files produced in 2011–2018 are likely to require substantial remediation, as 'accessibility principles were not still well understood'.[32] The digital divide is further accentuated by print-only publications, with countries like Lithuania revealing that on average only 14 per cent of books were released in an ebook format between 2010 and 2019 (Grigas & Gudinavičius 2023). This statistic underscores the mammoth task facing publishers in remediating their backlist.

Building upon the complex landscape of digital accessibility, the technological ecosystem presents publishers with a dynamic and ever-shifting challenge of maintaining compatibility and relevance across evolving platforms, standards, and formats. As technology advances, accessibility standards and guidelines need to adapt. The introduction of new devices, operating systems, and software creates a perpetual challenge of ensuring compatibility with assistive technologies. This technological arms race demands more than mere adaptation – it requires a fundamental reimagining of content creation and preservation strategies. For example, EPUB Accessibility 1.1 specification will need to be revised as new versions of WCAG are released, which means that the forward compatibility of content is likely to remain an issue.

Gregorio Pellegrino's critical observation on the W3C forum highlights a fundamental structural limitation: 'EPUBs are normally "static" documents that are not updated after being published (except on rare occasions).'[33] This characteristic creates a significant vulnerability in the rapidly evolving technological ecosystem. Publishers are confronted with

---

[32] www.abelab.eu/outcomes/backlist_data/.

[33] https://github.com/w3c/epub-specs/issues/1459.

a multifaceted mandate: they must simultaneously develop forward-looking workflows and ensure the ongoing compatibility of both front and backlist publications across mainstream and assistive technologies.

Copyright Concerns

The intricate landscape of digital accessibility reveals another critical dimension of complexity: the fundamental tension between technological innovation and long-standing intellectual property paradigms.

Copyright concerns have emerged as a profound philosophical and practical challenge for publishers, representing a deep-seated conflict between traditional print culture and the transformative potential of digital accessibility. The core of this tension, as Kevin Carey perceptively observes, lies in the 'direct conflict between document integrity and accessibility' (Carey 2012, 11). The idea of releasing files that can be manipulated by readers to suit their reading needs is an unnerving idea for an industry still committed to the 'typographical fixity' of 'print culture' in which the text is fixed and immutable (Eisenstein 1979, 71–88, 113–19), and relatively expensive to copy. The digital revolution fundamentally disrupts this model, creating files that are not only easily sharable, but also adaptable, allowing readers to dynamically modify their reading experience through reflowable EPUB formats.

To address this commercial concern, many publishers utilise digital rights management (DRM) systems. Paradoxically, DRM technologies frequently impede the legitimate use of ebooks by readers, including those with print disability, preventing crucial format shifting and rendering many assistive technologies ineffective (Hall 2013, 144). In 2012, Tor, a science fiction publisher, removed DRM in response to authors and readers wanting the ability to move books between various ereaders – a decision that inadvertently enhanced accessibility for people with print disability as well.

Publishers have also been concerned about the security of digital files shared with alternative format producers (Bowes III 2018), worrying that it 'would lead to "leakage" and piracy' (House et al. 2018, 32). Remarkably, specialised digital formats like DAISY and Braille Ready Format (BRF) emerged partially as a strategic response to rights-holders' concerns. As

Paul Harpur notes, these formats 'were created, in part, to enable persons with print disabilities to use their adaptive technology more effectively, and in part to reduce concerns from rights-holders that there would be leakage from the special case of print-disabled readers to the wider population' (Harpur 2017, 13). This approach represents a nuanced attempt to balance intellectual property protection with accessibility needs, acknowledging the legitimate requirements of print-disabled readers while mitigating broader distribution risks.

Is Accessibility 'Good' for Publishers?

Beyond the challenges of implementation, the strategic imperative of digital accessibility extends far beyond mere compliance, representing a transformative opportunity for publishers to redefine their market positioning and social impact. Digital accessibility emerges as a multifaceted strategic asset, transcending traditional perspectives of regulatory compliance to become a powerful lever for organisational innovation and market differentiation. Kogan Page, a publisher of academic and professional business books, is a good example of an organisation that heavily invested in born-accessible book production process, winning the IPG Digital Publishing Award in 2020 and the ABC International Excellence Award for Accessible Publishing in 2022.[34]

Kogan's success story aligns with broader industry perspectives on accessibility as a business advantage. The World Wide Web Consortium's Web Accessibility Initiative (W3C WAI) articulates a compelling business case, positioning accessibility not as a burden but as a strategic advantage that minimises legal risks, amplifies organisational branding, expands market reach, and catalyses innovative practices (W3C WAI 2018). All these benefits are relevant to the publishing industry, as many countries have regulations and standards in place that require digital content to be accessible to people with disability.

The strategic dimensions of accessibility implementation extend well beyond risk mitigation. Compliance with national and international accessibility regulations will serve as a critical protective mechanism, helping

[34] www.koganpage.com/accessibility.

publishers avoid legal issues and potential fines, a reality that becomes even more significant with the implementation of the EAA. Moreover, many procurement frameworks now explicitly require digital content accessibility, transforming it from an optional enhancement to a fundamental market entry requirement. This shift repositions accessibility from a peripheral consideration to a core competitive differentiator (Hurix 2023, PAAG n.d.).

Perhaps most compellingly, accessibility aligns with the evolving narrative of corporate social responsibility (CSR) in publishing. As Alison Jones (2015) observes, CRS initiatives in publishing have increasingly centred on the core mission 'on literacy and getting content to readers in the most accessible way' (Jones 2015). This approach repositions accessibility not merely as a technical requirement but as a profound ethical commitment to inclusive knowledge dissemination, potentially enhancing brand reputation and demonstrating a publisher's dedication to social equity. Taylor and Francis is an example of publisher with accessibility clearly seen as part of its corporate responsibility initiatives.[35]

As the publishing industry grapples with the strategic dimensions of accessibility, the economic potential of inclusive publishing emerges as a nuanced and compelling narrative of market transformation. While the potential market expansion through born-accessible publications has been a recurring topic of conversation (for example, AIPI 2019a, 10–12), the reality presents a more complex economic landscape. Simon Mellins (2024) cautions against overstating the increase in sales as an argument for accessibility implementation, highlighting that many individuals with print disability rely on free access via specialised libraries. This dependency reveals a critical market failure: the current ecosystem systematically constrains consumer choice and economic participation. The fundamental challenge extends beyond mere publication accessibility, requiring a comprehensive reimagining of digital distribution platforms. Currently, individuals with print disability face significant barriers in discovering and purchasing digital books, with accessible distribution platforms and

---

[35] https://taylorandfrancis.com/about/corporate-responsibility/accessibility-at-taylor-francis/.

comprehensive accessibility metadata remaining rare exceptions (see the Fondazione LIA's catalogue) rather than industry standards.

The concept of disability as a viable market segment is not a novel insight, but a strategic opportunity that has been progressively recognised since the late twentieth century. The term 'handicapitalism', coined by Joshua Prager in his 1999 *Wall Street Journal* article, represented a paradigm shift in economic thinking. Prager's seminal observation challenged prevailing perception, arguing that '[p]eople with disabilities shouldn't be viewed as charity cases or regulatory burdens, but rather as profitable marketing targets'. This perspective finds powerful contemporary validation in the UK's 'Purple Pound' phenomenon. With over 14 million disabled people commanding a combined spending power of £274 billion, this market segment demonstrates not just economic significance, but a remarkable brand loyalty to organisations committed to genuine inclusivity.[36]

As the global landscape of digital accessibility unfolds, the sheer magnitude of potential readers with print disability emerges as a profound, yet often overlooked, market opportunity. Estimating the prevalence of print disability globally presents a complex methodological challenge, characterised by significant variations in definitional approaches and data collection across different countries and organisations. The most comprehensive statistics are available for blindness and vision impairment, and these numbers indicate just how many people may be affected by print disability. The World Health Organization's 2019 report estimated that 'at least 2.2 billion people around the world have a vision impairment or blindness', a figure projected to grow due to 'population growth and ageing, along with behavioural and lifestyle changes, and urbanization' (WHO 2019, xi). To give another example, most studies estimate that between 3 and 7 per cent of people have dyslexia, based on scoring significantly below average on reading tests. Prevalence estimations are higher if the criteria are less strict (Wagner et al. 2020). These statistics represent not merely a demographic metric, but a compelling call to reimagine inclusive publishing strategies that have historically marginalised a substantial portion of potential readers.

[36] https://wearepurple.org.uk/about-us-purple/.

Moreover, empirical research reveals that individuals with print disability demonstrate remarkably robust and engaged reading behaviours. A landmark study by Creaser and colleagues uncovered a striking insight: people who are blind or partially sighted read more than sighted readers: 95 per cent read at least once a week for pleasure, in comparison to 74 per cent in the general population in the UK (Creaser et al. 2012, 16). Australian data further substantiates this trend, with 88 per cent of respondents with print disability reporting that they love or like to read, compared to 75 per cent of the general Australian population relaying that they read or listen to at least one book a year. The reading intensity is particularly noteworthy: 19 per cent of people with print disability read 6 or more books per month, 17 per cent read 4–5 books, and 35 per cent read 2–3 books. The remaining 29 per cent read one or fewer books each month (Australia Reads 2021; Mrva-Montoya 2022b). While these outcomes may have been biased, as both studies of people with print disability targeted book readers in the first place, publishers are missing out on potential sales by ignoring this market.

But, of course, the audience for accessible content is made up of many more people than just those who have no or low vision, or have a medical diagnosis of print disability. Beyond those with permanent, long- or short-term print disability, accessible content is also useful for users affected by functional limitations (a term used in the EAA [4]) or situationally induced impairments and disabilities (SIIDs). This term, created in 2003, uses a disability framework to conceptualise 'how various situations, contexts, and environments negatively affect people's abilities to interact with computing systems' (Wobbrock 2019, 61). The use of this term is controversial and has been seen to diminish 'the lived experiences of those with lifelong disabilities'. However, it has brought a useful perspective, showing that 'everyone experiences limits to their abilities ... when interacting with technology in dynamic situations, contexts, or environments' and highlighting the need to focus on 'designing for all users and their abilities – for what they can do in a given situation, and not what they cannot do' (Wobbrock 2019, 61).

This expansive understanding of accessibility challenges traditional narratives of disability by highlighting the contextual and fluid nature of human capability. Poor lighting, cognitive load, multilingual contexts, or multitasking-type activities (such as driving) can affect a person's ability to read books in print, so the ability to switch to another format is helpful. Many accessibility considerations are useful for readers who are not fluent in the dominant language (who benefit from the ability to hear the text spoken) or are multitasking (such as truck drivers, who are an important new audience for audiobooks). In fact, the audio format, which was originally produced to cater for blind veterans in the wake of both world wars, has become an alternative and increasingly popular way to 'read' books for sighted readers. What began as a specialised solution has evolved into a mainstream alternative, demonstrating how accessibility-driven innovations can create unexpected benefits for broader populations. Research increasingly supports this perspective, with scholars like Persson et al. arguing that accessible information and communication technology products and services (and this includes books in digital formats) are 'of a much wider importance than only for individuals with a disability. The benefits can be experienced by most stakeholders' (Persson et al. 2015, 506).

The pervasive nature of accessibility features reveals a profound truth: inclusive design is not a niche accommodation, but a universal approach that benefits all users. Accessible ebook and audiobook files are not just alternative formats, but technologically superior solutions that are more usable for all readers. According to Booknet Canada's 2018 survey on the use of ebooks, 'approximately half of all digital readers use accessibility features of some kind' when reading ebooks. This widespread adoption demonstrates that accessibility features are not marginal adaptations, but essential tools that fundamentally improve interaction with content. These features may include changing the typeface, font size, or text orientation; using night mode, screen magnification, or a screen reader; or adjusting colours (Harkonen 2018). Such versatility speaks to a broader understanding of user needs that transcends traditional notions of disability.

The evolving discourse on accessibility challenges narrow conceptualisations of disability, positioning it as a critical lens for understanding human diversity and technological design. As Ria Cheyenne argues in her 2019 book *Disability, Literature and Genre*, 'Disability studies has long sought to achieve recognition of the fact that disability is not a niche or minority interest, but a topic of vital importance to all people, whatever their disability status'. It is a fundamental aspect of human experience with universal relevance. The provocative term TAB ('temporarily able-bodied') serves as a powerful reminder that 'all people will become disabled if they live long enough' (Cheyne 2019, 12). This perspective re-contextualises accessibility not as a specialised service, but as a fundamental approach to design that anticipates the diverse and changing capabilities of all users. Accessibility considerations inherently benefit multiple groups – older adults, multilingual communities, individuals with situational limitations – thereby creating more flexible, intuitive, and inclusive technological environments.

To summarise, the advantages for publishers are evident. Investing in accessibility encourages publishers to stay up-to-date with the latest technologies and design principles, drives innovation in content delivery, and fosters a culture of adaptability. As Matthew Rubery notes, 'Media historians have long recognized the link between disability and invention' (Rubery 2016, 60). As well as talking books, innovations have included the typewriter, telephone, text-to-speech, email, and voice controls (Girma 2017). The question is no longer whether publishers should implement accessibility but how to do so effectively, and this is where collaboration with other stakeholders becomes crucial.

Working with Disability Organisations

Working with disability organisations represents a critical strategic approach to transforming content accessibility, highlighting the indispensable role of collaborative innovation. Historically, organisations in the disability sector have led the move towards improving access to content for people with print disability, often working against significant systemic barriers. Publishers now have an unprecedented opportunity to make disability organisations' work much easier by providing them with content in digital formats, even though the current legal instruments do not necessarily require them to do so. Reassuringly, this seems to be happening. Benetech's impressive achievement of engaging over 1,000 publishers in donating digital files to Bookshare® exemplifies the potential of such collaborative approaches.[37]

---

[37] www.bookshare.org/cms/partners/publishers/publisher-partners.

The critical importance of timely provision of suitable files becomes particularly evident in educational contexts where access can mean the difference between inclusion and exclusion. A 2020 survey of alternative-format producers in Australia revealed a stark reality: the length time required to produce an accessible format can vary from a mere one week to more than six months. This is a far cry from the same time, same format, same cost ideal. Apart from the time it takes to get a file from the publisher, other key variables include the type of source file, the size and complexity of the book, and the type of output produced. By faster turnaround and the provision of suitable files (ideally native files such as Adobe InDesign, Adobe Illustrator, EPUB or MS Word) via a digital transfer, publishers can dramatically reduce conversion time and cost (Mrva-Montoya 2020b, 19–20, 23), transforming what has historically been a cumbersome process into a streamlined, inclusive workflow.

Strategic partnerships between disability organisations and publishing industry bodies have also emerged as a transformative mechanism for advancing inclusive publishing practices. These collaborations are not merely symbolic gestures but represent sophisticated, pragmatic approaches to systemic change. The UK's 2020 report on implementing and scaling up inclusive business practices provides compelling evidence asserting that 'partnerships and peer-to-peer learning are the most effective ways that multinational businesses use to learn how to transform business practices to become more responsible, sustainable, and inclusive' (Lucas 2020, 2).

Such partnerships create virtuous cycles of knowledge exchange, where disability organisations provide crucial lived-experience insights, and publishers contribute technological and design expertise. This symbiotic relationship goes beyond traditional corporate social responsibility, representing a fundamental reimagining of content production as an inherently inclusive process. Actively engaging with alternative-format producers and other print-disability organisations is crucial to counteract the lack of accessibility knowledge among publishing professionals (see, for example, NNELS n.d.). These entities have a deep understanding of the needs of people with lived experience of print disability, their requirements, and the relevant accessibility laws and technical standards. With their extensive knowledge of assistive technologies, both hardware and software, and accessible format production, they can assist publishers in both testing products and incorporating feedback from individuals with print disability – the key stakeholders in the accessibility implementation process.

Beyond broad cross-sector initiatives, targeted collaborations between individual publishers and print-disability organisations are increasingly demonstrating the transformative potential of direct, intentional partnerships targeting the implementation of inclusive publishing workflows or the production of individual titles. Sydney University Press' collaboration with the Royal Institute for Blind and Deaf Children (currently NextSense) and Infogrid Pacific in 2018 exemplifies this approach. NextSense provided critical guidance and feedback on file requirements and facilitated user-testing with readers with print disability.[38] Similarly, Penguin Random House Canada's collaboration with NNELS represents another milestone in inclusive publishing, demonstrating a commitment to simultaneous multi-format releases. By publishing Jamie Oliver's *5 Ingredients Mediterranean*, simultaneously in print and braille (BookNet Canada 2023), the publisher challenged traditional publishing models and signalled a profound shift towards genuinely inclusive content strategies. These examples illuminate how targeted collaborations can transform accessibility from a compliance requirement to a robust, user-centred approach to content creation.

Global Developments in Accessibility Implementation

The evolution of accessibility initiatives globally reveals a powerful narrative of collaborative innovation. Much of the work has been led by the DAISY Consortium, which was formed in May 1996 to facilitate the transition from analogue to digital talking books. Following the development of DAISY (Digital Accessible Information SYstem), the consortium has positioned itself as a comprehensive ecosystem architect, bringing together publishers, technology organisations, and individuals with print disability to fundamentally reimagine content accessibility. The consortium's multifaceted approach encompasses developing robust standards and guidelines, raising critical awareness about inclusive publishing, and

---

[38] https://sydneyuniversitypress.com.au/pages/accessibility.

supporting open standards that challenge traditional content production paradigms. Its technological innovations – including software such as Ace by DAISY (an accessibility checker for EPUB), Obi (an audiobook production tool for digital talking books), and WordToEPUB (an EPUB creation tool) demonstrate a sophisticated understanding of accessibility as a dynamic, technologically mediated process. The consortium also created the Simple Manual Accessibility Reporting Tool (SMART), and provides consultancy services and training.[39] By maintaining platforms such as the Google-funded Inclusive Publishing website[40] and the knowledge base,[41] and fostering international collaborations such as with Libri Italiani Accessibili Fondazione (known as Fondazione LIA) in Italy, DAISY has created a global infrastructure for accessible content development.

The World Intellectual Property Organization's (WIPO) Accessible Books Consortium (ABC) represents another key organisation in the global accessibility landscape, building upon foundational work of an earlier Enabling Technologies project, undertaken by EDItEUR, the Royal National Institute of Blind People (RNIB), and the DAISY Consortium. Launched in 2014 to support the implementation of the Marrakesh Treaty, the project facilitates access to accessible digital books via the ABC Global Book Service and provides guidance for publishers producing mainstream accessible econtent as exemplified by *Accessible Publishing: Best Practice Guidelines* (Hilderley 2013 [2011]). The ABC also helps with capacity building in developing countries, and promotes the production of born-accessible publications. Through the Charter for Accessible Publishing, the ABC has developed an innovative mechanism that encourages organisations to embed accessibility as a core organisational value, requiring signatories to develop an accessibility policy, implement inclusive publishing practices, raise accessibility awareness, and actively collaborate with other organisations.[42] The annual ABC International Excellence Award further

[39] https://daisy.org/activities/.
[40] https://inclusivepublishing.org/about-the-inclusive-publishing-hub/; House et al. 2018, 33.
[41] http://kb.daisy.org/publishing/docs/.
[42] www.accessiblebooksconsortium.org/portal/en/charter.html.

amplifies this approach by creating a global recognition system that celebrates 'outstanding leadership and achievements in advancing the accessibility of digital publications for persons who are print disabled'.[43]

While these global organisations provide leadership and support, the publishing industry itself is increasingly leading the transition towards inclusive publishing workflows. By working with stakeholders in the disability and technology sectors, the industry is driving meaningful change that goes beyond national borders. A number of interesting cross-sector and cross-border collaborations and partnerships have been taking place in Europe, North America, Australia and Aotearoa New Zealand. These efforts represent a paradigm shift from isolated, compliance-driven approaches to holistic, innovation-driven strategies that recognise accessibility as a fundamental aspect of content design, production, and distribution.

Europe

The Italian publishing sector's transformative approach offers a compelling model of systemic accessibility innovation. In 2011, the Associazione Italiana Editori (AIE), with the support of the Italian government's Ministry for Cultural Heritage and Activities, started a project to create a catalogue of accessible books. In 2014, AIE set up Fondazione LIA to ensure the continuity of the project.[44] Following a pioneering approach, the foundation has worked on the accessibility of the whole publishing ecosystem, rather than just ebook files. Over time, it developed an industrial-scale approach to accessibility implementation by offering consultancy and services that assist publishers and all other stakeholders in the book value chain to adapt their production and distribution workflows for ebook and websites. By offering nuanced, scaled consultancy services – ranging from training and support to file-conformance checking – the foundation has created a financially sustainable model of accessibility implementation. The organisation's pricing structure (from a few hundred to thousands of euros annually),[45] which depends on the size of the publishing programme,

---

[43] www.accessiblebooksconsortium.org/publishing/en/.

[44] www.fondazionelia.org/en/who-we-are/the-foundation/.

[45] Cristina Mussinelli and Lisa Molinari, personal communication, 7 February 2024.

demonstrates a sophisticated understanding of diverse organisational needs. The 'Reading in the Dark' programme further illustrates this holistic approach, using 'a highly experiential and engaging format to address themes as digital accessibility and the socio-cultural inclusion of people with visual disabilities',[46] and transforming accessibility from a technical challenge into a profound human experience.

Since the beginning, Fondazione LIA has strategically built partnerships with key international organisations that specialise in the development of standards and solutions for accessible reading. This deliberate network-building approach has yielded substantial intellectual and practical outcomes, generating a rich repository of guidelines, reports, and other resources.[47] Fondazione LIA is currently leading the 2024–2025 APACE (Accelerating Publishing Accessibility through Collaboration in Europe) network, which focuses on developing innovative 'methods for producing and distributing accessible ebooks' through collaboration and capacity building.[48] Through these efforts, Fondazione LIA is not merely responding to existing challenges but actively reshaping the technological and social infrastructures of publishing.

In the UK, the publishing sector's accessibility journey exemplifies a similar trajectory of institutional transformation, with the Publishers Association's Accessibility Action Group (AAG) serving as a pioneering mechanism for systemic change. Established in 2010 to support the development and distribution of accessible publications, the AAG has operated as a comprehensive catalyst for accessibility implementation, simultaneously investigating developments in legislation, policy, and technological developments, while developing guidance and best practice for publishers.[49] The group was renamed the Publishing Accessibility Action Group (PAAG) and became a separate organisation from the Publishers Association in 2022.

---

[46] www.fondazionelia.org/en/what-we-do/reading-in-the-dark/.

[47] See for example: Tools for Born Accessible Publishing. www.fondazionelia.org/en/resources/tools-for-born-accessible-publishing/.

[48] www.fondazionelia.org/en/project/2024-apace-accelerating-publishing-accessibility-through-collaboration-in-europe/.

[49] www.publishers.org.uk/about-us/groups/.

The new PAAG website provides a platform for publishers at any stage of the accessibility journey to make meaningful commitment (by signing a charter) and access critical resources.[50]

The Netherlands' journey towards inclusive publishing represents a sophisticated model of institutional collaboration, built upon a foundational partnership established in the 1980s between the Dutch Publishers Association (Mediafederatie), Dedicon (an alternative format producer), and the National Library (Koninklijke Bibliotheek). This early commitment to accessible publication of copyright-protected works laid the groundwork for a more comprehensive, proactive approach to inclusive publishing. In 2016, Dedicon strategically initiated a series of round-table discussions to explore the adoption of born-accessible publishing practices within the mainstream industry. These discussions resulted in the release of measures and guidelines for publishers, 'ordered by effect per reading disability and ease of implementation', and a quick-start guide to accessible publishing (Verboom 2019, 4).

The Dutch government support for inclusive publishing funded critical initiatives that extend far beyond isolated interventions. The accessible publishing project (FondsXL), and Toegankelijk Publiceren aan de Bron 1 [Accessible Publishing at the Source] (2018–2019) and Toegankelijk Publiceren aan de Bron 2 (2021–2022) projects represent a comprehensive, multi-year strategy designed to incrementally build awareness, develop training programmes and construct a knowledge base.[51] Dedicon's international collaborations, with BrailleNet (France) and Johannes Kepler Universität Linz (Austria), in the Supporting Inclusive Digital Publishing through Training (SIDPT), a partnership co-funded by the European Union's Erasmus+ Programme underscore the transnational nature of accessibility innovation. By developing a learning platform, Inclusive Publishing in Practice, with content in English, French, Dutch, and German,[52] the initiative creates a multilingual infrastructure for knowledge exchange.

---

[50] www.paag.uk/, PAAG 2023.

[51] Verboom 2019, 4–5; DAISY Consortium 2021a; see also www.inclusiefpubliceren.nl/.

[52] www.inclusivepublishinginpractice.org.

In Germany, the work on accessibility implementation in the industry has been galvanised by the early adoption of the EAA into national legislation. In 2020, an industry taskforce was convened to work with publishers in Austria and Switzerland, focusing on producing industry documentation, training, and webinars.[53]

In the Scandinavian countries, the Nordic Inclusive Publishing Initiative[54] was established in 2019 to raise awareness of accessibility and make the shift to 'inclusive publishing based on universal design of products and services' in Denmark, Finland, Iceland, Norway, and Sweden. Further south, in Poland, in 2016 the government funded the development of the accessible online platform IBUK Libra Light, aimed specifically at readers with print disability. The platform hosts publications as EPUB and MP3 files and works with NVDA and other assistive technologies,[55] providing a concrete example of how targeted technological solutions can dramatically improve reading experiences for individuals with disabilities.

In addition to these national initiatives, two Europe-wide projects demonstrate a strategic approach to advancing accessibility implementation in the publishing industry. The European Digital Reading Lab (EDR Lab) was established in 2015 to support European publishers in 'the development and use of open, interoperable and accessible technologies'. The organisation's multifaceted approach is particularly noteworthy. By developing and maintaining open source software like Readium for EPUB3 publications and Thorium Reader, EDR Lab provides concrete technological solutions that lower barriers to digital accessibility. The annual Digital Publishing Summit further amplifies its impact, creating a crucial forum for knowledge exchange, collaboration, and strategic planning among publishers, technologists, and accessibility experts.[56]

Complementing the EDR Lab's technological initiatives, the European Inclusive Publishing Forum, commissioned by the DAISY Consortium in

---

[53] DAISY Consortium 2021b; see also www.boersenverein.de/beratung-service/barrierefreiheit/.
[54] https://nipi.care.
[55] https://pzn.org.pl/niewidomi-z-wlasna-platforma-ksiazek/.
[56] www.edrlab.org/about/.

November 2020, represents a strategic response to the EAA. This network is a proactive mechanism that aims to 'to share expertise and information, reduce duplication, and identify a path forward to achieve Inclusive Publishing maximizing the opportunity of the European Accessibility Act'.[57] By bringing together diverse stakeholders, the forum creates a synergistic environment that can accelerate the implementation of accessibility standards across Europe.

These initiatives showcase a sophisticated, multi-layered approach to addressing accessibility challenges in the publishing industry. Rather than relying solely on legislative mandates, they combine technological innovation, collaborative networking, and knowledge sharing. This holistic strategy suggests a deep understanding that true inclusivity requires more than top-down regulations – it demands active, collaborative engagement from multiple sectors.

By establishing robust infrastructure, facilitating expertise exchange, and providing practical technological solutions, these European projects set a global benchmark for inclusive publishing. They represent not just a regional effort, but a potential model for international approaches to digital accessibility.

North America

While operating under a different legal framework from the European Union, North America's approach to accessibility implementation showcases a similarly robust and innovative strategy, with distinct variations across nations.

The Association of Canadian Publishers and eBOUND Canada (2020) carried out one of most comprehensive research projects to date, supported by government funding (discussed in the next section). This research project was particularly significant for its collaborative methodology, bringing together diverse perspectives in the book value chain. The reader perspective of the survey was carried out in collaboration with the National Network for Equitable Library Service (NNELS), an organisation

---

[57] https://daisy.org/activities/projects/european-inclusive-publishing-forum/.

Inclusive Publishing and the Quest for Reading Equity 51

which maintains a digital repository of accessible titles available through Canadian public libraries.

NNELS has emerged as a pivotal institution in Canada's accessible publishing landscape. Since 2019, NNELS has been organising the annual Accessible Publishing Summit, a critical forum where representatives from the ebook production and distribution chain work on developing best practices and techniques for accessible publishing (Brady & Levy-Pinto 2019).

In the United States, the publishing industry's approach to accessibility is characterised by both research-driven and market-oriented initiatives. The Book Industry Study Group (BISG) exemplifies this approach by researching market trends and issues, maintaining standardised best practices, and providing advice and training to the industry on digital workflows and accessibility.[58]

Complementing BISG's systemic approach, Benetech, a not-for-profit social enterprise organisation, has emerged as a transformative force in driving accessibility implementation within the publishing industry. Its Global Certified Accessible™ (GCA) programme[59] represents an innovative certification mechanism that guides publishers in accessibility implementation (discussed in Chapter 3). To support the distribution of certified books, Benetech and VitalSource developed Benetech's Born Accessible Ebook Store, where students can buy or rent accessible books. The Bookshelf® reading app further enhances this offering, integrating interactive features specifically designed to support student learning, thus demonstrating how technological innovation can directly translate to enhanced educational opportunities.[60] This platform is a strategic intervention in the accessible publishing ecosystem. These North American initiatives collectively represent a multidimensional approach to inclusive publishing.

Australia and Aotearoa New Zealand

As global efforts towards accessible publishing continue to evolve, the approaches in Australia and Aotearoa New Zealand demonstrate a distinctive

---

[58] www.bisg.org/products/bisg-guide-to-accessible-publishing–cheat-sheets.

[59] https://bornaccessible.benetech.org/global-certified-accessible/.

[60] https://benetechaccessiblebooks.vitalsource.com/.

model of collaborative, grassroots-driven accessibility initiatives that blend long-standing advocacy with innovative, multi-stakeholder strategies.

The Round Table on Information Access for People with Print Disability stands as a pioneering organisation, with a remarkable legacy spanning over four decades. Established in 1981, the Round Table has been instrumental in creating a comprehensive ecosystem for accessible information production. Its multifaceted approach goes far beyond simple advocacy, actively producing standards and guidelines, facilitating critical dialogue between users and providers of accessible information, and supporting research across Australia and Aotearoa New Zealand.[61] This sustained commitment has been crucial in developing a nuanced understanding of accessibility challenges and potential solutions.

A significant milestone in Australia's inclusive publishing journey came in November 2016 with the establishment of the Marrakesh Treaty Forum. This landmark gathering, under the leadership of the Australian Publishers Association, was remarkable for its unprecedented collaborative approach, bringing together the representatives of the publishing industry, libraries, copyright organisations, disability associations, government, and accessible-format providers. The forum's explicit goal to 'foster a collaborative, consultative and consensus-based approach' to making published materials accessible represented a paradigm shift in addressing accessibility challenges.[62] The forum, later renamed the Australian Inclusive Publishing Initiative (AIPI), exemplifies a strategic and systematic approach to improving publishing accessibility. Its annual meetings provided space for brainstorming, knowledge exchange, and collective problem-solving. The tangible outcomes of these meetings, such as a website with case studies and the publication of two guides (AIPI 2019a, 2019b), demonstrate the practical effectiveness of this collaborative model.

The work of AIPI was continued under the umbrella of the Institute of Professional Editors (IPEd), who in late 2020 set up the Accessibility Initiative Working Party in response to the need for further guidelines and training. This work resulted in the release of 'Books without Barriers: A

---

[61] https://printdisability.org/. [62] https://aipi.com.au/.

Practical Guide to Inclusive Publishing' (Ganner et al. 2023), a comprehensive framework for understanding and implementing inclusive publishing. The revision of the 'IPEd Standards for Editing Practice' (IPEd 2024) is another noteworthy development. By incorporating a strong focus on editing for accessibility, diversity, equity, and inclusion, these standards represent a transformative approach to industry self-regulation. The integration of accessibility into editing training programmes and the accreditation exam for editors working in Australia and Aotearoa New Zealand signals a fundamental cultural shift within publishing and the editing profession. What makes these initiatives particularly powerful is their holistic and collaborative nature. Rather than viewing accessibility implementation as a compliance requirement, these approaches treat it as an integral part of professional practice and social responsibility aligned with the human rights model of disability.

The global landscape of accessible publishing extends far beyond the regions previously discussed, revealing a rich tapestry of initiatives that demonstrate the universal importance of reading equity across diverse cultural and economic contexts. While the focus of this overview of global initiatives focuses on Europe, North America, and Australia and Aotearoa New Zealand, work on accessibility implementation has also been happening in other parts of the world, including Brazil, India,[63] Kenia (EducationLinks 2019), Mexico (Bermúdez 2024), the United Arab Emirates,[64] and undoubtedly many others, as demonstrated by the list of signatories to the ABC Charter for Accessible Publishing.[65] The charter serves as a powerful testament to the global nature of this movement. It illustrates that accessibility is not a peripheral concern but a fundamental aspect of modern publishing.

Funding the Move to Inclusive Publishing

The financial landscape of inclusive publishing represents a complex ecosystem of challenges, opportunities, and strategic interventions that go far beyond simple monetary support.

---

[63] www.chetana.org.in/armlibrary. [64] https://kalimatfoundation.ae/.
[65] www.accessiblebooksconsortium.org/publishing/abc_charter_for_accessible_publishing_signatories.

Funding the transition to inclusive publishing, where the production of accessible formats is integrated into mainstream publishing, is not merely a financial challenge but a transformation that requires a sophisticated understanding of the publishing industry's structural complexities. Accessibility implementation is particularly challenging giving the vast disparities in organisational size, resources, and capabilities that characterise the publishing landscape.

Larger publishing companies present a paradoxical scenario. While they have substantial financial resources that they could theoretically dedicate to the implementation process and training, and they are more likely to be involved in corporate responsibility initiatives (Jones 2015), their bureaucratic structures often become significant barriers. These complex organisational machines can be remarkably unwieldy and sometimes ineffective, making resource allocations and strategic shifts time-consuming. The process of securing buy-in across multiple departments can become a labyrinthine challenge that delays meaningful progress.

Conversely, smaller companies face a fundamentally different set of constraints. They are nimbler, but they have limited human and financial resources, which impacts how much money they can invest in implementing inclusive publishing workflows. This resource scarcity creates a significant implementation barrier, potentially marginalising smaller publishers in the accessibility transformation.

The EAA demonstrates a nuanced understanding of these challenges by explicitly acknowledging the lower capacity of smaller companies to implement accessibility measures. By exceptions for these businesses, as discussed in Chapter 1, the EAA recognises that a one-size-fits-all approach is ineffective in driving industry-wide accessibility implementation.

Government interventions, as exemplified by countries such as Canada, Italy and the Netherlands, have emerged as critical catalysts in accelerating industry's transition to inclusive practices. The Canadian example is particularly illuminating. Consistent with its long history of policy interventions aimed at supporting Canadian-owned and -controlled book publishers, which dates back to the 1970s (Boggs 2010), in March 2019 the federal government announced 'an investment of $22.8 million over five years for the development of an initiative to support the sustainable production and distribution of accessible digital books by Canadian independent publishers'. The Accessible Digital Books Initiative aimed to support collaborative projects focusing on 'increasing accessible publishing capacity in Canada, helping market and showcase accessible books, developing and promoting best practices and implementing industry standards and certification' (Government of Canada 2022).

This funding went far beyond mere financial support. It enabled comprehensive research, developed critical training programmes, and enabled many publishers in Canada to implement inclusive publishing workflows, including certification by Benetech (discussed in Chapter 3). The tangible outcome is striking – by June 2024, fifty-four out of eighty-two Benetech-certified organisations were from Canada, and another six Canadian publishers were certified through the International Publishing Program partner eBOUND Canada.[66] This achievement is especially significant given that 78 per cent of Canadian-owned publishers are small firms with ten or fewer employees (Nordicity & ACP 2018).

While funding for the Accessible Digital Books Initiative has not been extended, the Canadian Benetech certification pilot will continue to run. Publishers will be able to get yearly check-ins, and new publishers sign up for certification, for the foreseeable future. Moreover, a new Equitable Access to Reading Program by Employment and Social Development Canada (ESDC) announced in 2022 has a substantial budget of $21 million to be spent over three years, starting in 2024–2025 (NNELS 2022).

It will be interesting to see how the funding model will evolve in the coming years, and to study its long-term impact on industry practices. While the industry-wide progress in accessibility implementation is clear, over-reliance on government funding can be risky for organisations, particularly if future funding is reduced or discontinued. This dependence can potentially hinder the development of sustainable, self-regulated accessibility practices within the industry. The future of inclusive publishing funding will likely require a dynamic, adaptive approach that balances external support with internal industry transformation. It's not just about providing financial resources, but about creating sustainable ecosystems that inherently value and implement accessibility.

---

[66] https://bornaccessible.benetech.org/certified-publishers/.

This chapter has demonstrated that the transition to inclusive publishing requires overcoming significant barriers around knowledge, capacity, cost, and copyright concerns. However, the business case for accessibility is compelling – it expands market reach, enhances brand reputation, reduces legal risks, and creates better products for all users through universal design principles. The successful implementation of inclusive publishing practices relies heavily on strategic collaborations between publishers, disability organisations, and industry bodies, as evidenced by transformative initiatives across Europe, North America, Australia, and beyond. Government funding has also played a crucial role in supporting this transition, particularly for smaller publishers with limited resources. Chapter 3 explores how organisations have been operationalising these insights by embedding accessibility principles throughout their policies, workflows, and quality assurance processes.

3 Implementing Inclusive Publishing

The implementation of inclusive publishing practices requires more than technical solutions – it demands a fundamental reimagining of how books are created, produced, and distributed. While the industry has historically focused on visual presentation and print-first workflows, the shift towards inclusive publishing practices requires publishers to reconceptualise books as content that can be accessed through multiple modalities. This chapter examines how publishers can implement this transformation systematically and sustainably, arguing that successful implementation requires coordinated change across organisational culture, workflows, quality assurance processes, and supply chain management.

The publishing industry's journey towards accessibility has lagged behind other sectors, particularly the electronic and information technology industry. However, this delayed adoption offers an opportunity to learn from other industries' experiences while addressing publishing's unique challenges. These challenges include the industry's deeply embedded print-first mentality, the complexity of retrofitting extensive backlists, and the need to coordinate multiple stakeholders across a fragmented supply chain. Despite these obstacles, the imperative for change is clear: accessibility is not merely a technical requirement but a fundamental aspect of publishing's future relevance and sustainability.

Drawing on recent industry surveys, case studies, and emerging best practices, this chapter evaluates a comprehensive framework for implementing inclusive publishing. It begins by examining organisational strategies, including the crucial roles of accessibility champions, policy integration, and stakeholder engagement. The discussion then moves to practical aspects of workflow transformation, exploring how publishers have been shifting from retroactive accessibility fixes to born-accessible content creation. Quality assurance and certification emerge as critical components, not just for ensuring technical compliance but for building confidence among both publishers and readers. Finally, the chapter examines how accessibility implementation must extend beyond individual publishers to encompass the entire book supply chain, from metadata standards to retail platforms to ensure reading equity.

Throughout this analysis, the chapter demonstrates that successful implementation of inclusive publishing practices requires a holistic approach, driven by the human rights model of disability, that weaves accessibility into every aspect of publishing operations – or, as Tusler (2005) argues, into the very 'DNA of the company'. While such transformation presents significant challenges, the experience of early adopters shows that it is both achievable and increasingly essential for publishers' long-term success.

Strategic Framework for Organisational Transformation

Having established the urgent need for inclusive publishing, we can turn to proven frameworks for implementing systematic change. The information technology sector, despite its shorter history, offers valuable lessons for publishers seeking to embed accessibility into their operations. The findings from a 2002 survey conducted by Anthony Tusler on behalf of the World Institute of Disability are particularly relevant as they identify best practices (defined as 'process, procedure, system, or perspective') that can guide publishers in making their products and services accessible to people with disability.

At the organisational level, Tusler (2005) emphasises the critical role of an accessibility champion who can 'learn about disability'; liaise, coordinate work and mediate between 'the internal divisions and disability informants'; and 'use community-organizing strategies to create change'. This champion-led approach must be part of a broader strategy to transform organisational values and culture. Companies need to 'understand the needs and concerns of the disability community', involve people with disability in the product and process design, and 'include disability with other diversity efforts'. Crucially, organisations must also 'define the disability market', 'demonstrate the profitability of access', and 'tie access to mainstream product needs' – steps that align particularly well with publishers' existing expertise in market analysis and product development.

Most importantly, Tusler argues for fundamental transformation by 'weav[ing] accessibility into the DNA of the company'. This requires developing a strategic plan that aligns access accessibility implementation with the company's culture, values, and structure. The DNA metaphor emphasises how accessibility and universal design need to be incorporated into existing processes and practices, across all divisions of the company, in a sustainable way. Such deep integration demands active involvement from senior management, ongoing development of accessibility expertise through education and training, and the hiring of people with disability. These efforts must then be publicised internally and externally to promote accessible products, document progress, and further drive the change (Tusler 2005).

While Goggin and Newell raise valid concerns about the DNA concept for ignoring 'the social shaping of accessibility itself, as well as the complexity and contingency of corporate structure and practice', the publishing industry can benefit significantly from Tusler's systematic approach. As they note, 'bring[ing] about inclusive technology ... requires much coordination, commitment, and action between and among noncommercial as well as commercial sectors, institutions, and actors' (Goggin & Newell 2007, 162–63). The adoption of inclusive publishing practices demands this same level of coordination, perhaps even more so, given the industry's centuries-old tradition and complex stakeholder networks. Publishers must therefore adapt these frameworks thoughtfully, acknowledging both the unique challenges of their industry and the transformative potential of systematic accessibility implementation.

Accessibility Policy, Champions, and Communication

Moving from theoretical frameworks to practical implementation, successful publishers have been first establishing clear organisational structures and policies to drive change. The adoption of inclusive publishing workflows requires a company-wide commitment and engagement with each stakeholder involved in the publishing process, both internal and external. This systematic approach directly addresses Tusler's call for weaving accessibility into organisational DNA, while acknowledging the unique complexities of publishing operations.

Evidence from recent industry surveys underscores both the challenges and progress in this area. A 2020 survey of Australian publishers identified lack of leadership support as one of the key barriers to adoption, highlighting why executive leadership is essential to drive organisational pledge to accessibility, allocate resources, and sign off on accessibility policy (Mrva-Montoya 2020a, 22, 26). The critical role of accessibility champions, emphasised in Tusler's framework, has been validated by industry experience. As Stacy Scott notes, 'finding a suitably passionate individual is a key action' (Scott 2022, 695). The 2022 UK survey reveals encouraging progress, with 62 per cent of respondents reporting having dedicated accessibility roles or teams, including formal structures such as Bloomsbury's Accessibility Working Group, the Digital Accessibility Champions Network at Cambridge University Press (Alexander 2022, 700, 702; PAAG 2022) and the Accessibility Working Group at Taylor & Francis (Scott 2022, 691–92).

Such champions and teams serve as crucial bridges between internal departments and external stakeholders. Their success in forming partnerships with print-disability agencies, charities, and industry-based groups (Alexander 2022, 702) demonstrates how organisational commitment can extend beyond company boundaries to create broader systemic change. However, while dedicated accessibility roles are vital, the implementation process must permeate all organisational functions.

The comprehensive scope of accessibility implementation becomes clear when examining how it affects each department in a publishing house. Although the organisational structure of a publisher can vary depending on its scope, size, and specialisation, it typically comprises management, editorial, design and production, marketing and sales, rights and permissions, finance and human resources. Each of these roles touches on accessibility, including leadership, as already mentioned.

- The editorial department is responsible for creating a house accessibility style guide; contracting/briefing authors, editors, and illustrators; editing for accessibility; writing or editing alt text; and the creation of accessibility metadata.
- The design department is responsible for the design and layout of books and marketing collateral, ensuring that visual content, such as typography, colour schemes, and layout are usable by people with print disability.
- The production department is responsible for the creation of accessible formats (with appropriate metadata) and platforms, and quality assurance.

- The marketing and sales department is responsible for the dissemination of accessibility metadata and accessible distribution that is ensuring the website, marketing, and promotional campaigns are accessible (including book launch events).
- The rights and permissions department is responsible for providing files for conversion into alternative formats such as braille.
- The finance and accounting department directs resources to support accessibility implementation.
- The human resources department oversees the delivery of training, as well as the recruitment of staff, which should be inclusive of people with different disabilities.

The list of internal stakeholders involved in the publishing process shows the complexity of change required to adopt inclusive publishing practices. But, of course, this complexity is also present in the external environment. Publishing is an inherently collaborative endeavour, and many bigger and smaller publishing houses outsource various aspects of manuscript development and book production, or rely on third-party providers to produce books. All need to be briefed, consulted, and aligned with the accessibility commitment, from authors, freelance editors, and designers to platform providers to ebook conversion houses (Ganner et al. 2023, 34–37).

Across both internal and external production workflows, robust accessibility policies serve as a crucial foundation of organisational commitment to inclusive publishing. Organisational policies 'are the framework for taking actions', guiding the processes leading to 'proactive accessibility' across workflows, procurement, evaluation techniques, and compliance or quality-assurance monitoring (Lazar et al. 2015, 29–30). An organisation's policy should inform the development of briefs and guidelines for authors, staff, and vendors, to ensure best practice is followed throughout the publishing process.[67] The policy should also guide co-operation with disability agencies to facilitate a timely response to requests for digital files for specialised conversion.

---

[67] Ganner et al. 2023, 38; see also www.routledge.com/our-customers/authors/publishing-guidelines/accessible-content.

The importance of comprehensive policy extends beyond production to encompass all aspects of a publisher's presence. Everything 'around' the book also needs to be accessible – any publisher-owned platforms, marketing collateral, websites, catalogues, book and author events, and social media. Furthermore, following Tusler's emphasis on public commitment, publishers must articulate the 'accessibility story' by having accessibility statements on their websites. The impact of such transparency is evident in the ASPIRE project's work,[68] where accessibility statement scores have become a factor in library procurement decisions (Alexander 2022, 699), demonstrating the business value of public accessibility commitment.

Inclusive Publishing Workflows

While organisational policies provide the framework for change, their successful implementation depends on transforming publishing workflows. The industry's traditional reliance on a print-first workflow is problematic, as it is driven by the concept of 'content' and 'appearance' being intrinsically intertwined. This approach, deeply embedded in publishing culture, must evolve to meet accessibility requirements. A digital-first or format-neutral workflow, where content is properly structured from the beginning, and treated independently from the design, offers a more sustainable path forward. This shift in approach allows accessibility features to be automatically embedded throughout the production process, rather than retrofitted at the end.

The scope of this transformation extends beyond simple technical changes. As Simone Murray notes, all books 'encompass the dual dimensions of *text* (i.e. the words that are perceptible by readers) and *object* (i.e. the three-dimensional thing that can be bought, sold, archived or burnt)' (Murray 2020, 4, original italics). Inclusive publishing must address both dimensions, content and its presentation, and not only digital but also print formats. Each stage of the book creation process is affected, from writing to editing to design.

This comprehensive approach aligns with the UN CRPD's qualified call for universal design, which states that products should be 'usable by all

---

[68] www.textboxdigital.com/aspirelist-publishers.

people, *to the greatest extent possible*, without the need for adaptation or specialized design' (Art. 2; my italics). Similarly, the Inclusive Design Toolkit acknowledges that 'while inclusive design intends to extend the reach of mainstream products', it must balance commercial constraints with market needs.[69]

The practical implementation of these principles manifests in multiple ways. At the content level, publishers must ensure non-visual and inclusive language, such as replacing sight-dependent phrases like 'as shown in the figure below' with more inclusive alternative like 'as presented in figure 1'. Design considerations include colour-blindness-friendly palettes, and sufficient contrast between text and background (Ganner et al. 2023, 59–60, 141). Digital publications demand particular attention to ensure that 'all non-text content is also available in text'; the content is presented and operates in predictable ways; and the ebook file is machine-readable and usable by assistive devices and technology, and compatible with current and future technologies by using well-formed and standards-compliant markup and code (W3C WAI 2023). The digital files should be technically robust so that alternative-format providers can easily convert them into more specialised formats such as braille. The widespread adoption of reflowable EPUB3 has simplified this process as EPUB publications 'can be authored with a high degree of accessibility simply through the proper application of established Web accessibility techniques' (W3C 2017).

One of the more resource-intensive challenges lies in making non-textual elements accessible. They need to be accompanied by alternative (alt) text (and, in some cases, long text descriptions as well) so they can be read by assistive technologies. Alt text creation requires not just technical skill but deep understanding of context and often subject matter expertise. Success in this area increasingly depends on involving authors early in the process (Kasdorf 2018, 14; Ganner et al. 2023, 35). As Cooper et al. (2023, 65) observe, 'authors are not burdened by alt-text, so long as the rationale is clear and appropriate publisher support is available'. Moreover, Scott (2022, 694) also confirms that with the right support, authors 'provid[e] some wonderful, fully accessible content and enjoying doing so'.

---

[69] www.inclusivedesigntoolkit.com/whatis/whatis.html.

Similar considerations apply to audio and multimedia content: captions/subtitles (a text version of the audio that is shown synchronised in the media player), transcripts (a separate text version of the audio), and descriptions of visual information. They must be thoughtfully crafted to serve both accessibility needs and broader usability goals. WCAG recommends the use of 'integrated description' in which 'all the visual information that users need to understand the content is integrated in the main audio' (W3C WAI 2021). While captions and transcripts are typically aimed at individuals who are Deaf and those with hearing impairments, they also make content accessible to a broader audience by providing a visual representation of spoken, additional context; clarifying dialogue; and enhancing the learning experience by reinforcing the spoken audio. Transcripts are also useful for anyone who prefers to read the content or wants to quickly scan the information without watching the video.

The prevailing advice about the creation of alt text and audio descriptions calls for an objective and self-effacing approach, 'a neutral, unobtrusive act of translation that moves information from one medium into another'. However, Kleege and Wallin (2015) argue for the need to 'explore strategies that vary depending upon the context of audience, material, and critical and aesthetic goals' in the production of audio description. Similar factors should be considered when providing alt text in books. For example, descriptions of images in a children's book should be consistent with its narrative and visual aesthetics.

Whether written by authors or created by vendors or editorial staff, alt text, long descriptions, audio descriptions, transcripts, and captioning should go through the same editorial process as the rest of the manuscript, to assess their accuracy and relevance and to avoid the repetition of information already covered in the manuscript. It is therefore crucial that publishers think, plan, and assign responsibilities for the creation of alternative text and captions at the beginning of the publication process (Ganner et al. 2023, 35–36).

Despite the clear rationale for thinking about accessibility from the outset, and embedding it in the whole publishing process, some publishers still address accessibility considerations only at the end of the ebook production process. The approach taken with frontlist titles depends on how ebooks are produced (in-house or outsourced); whether the publisher relies on a print-first, digital-first, or format-neutral workflow; and the stage of the publisher's accessibility journey, with inclusive publishing practice being the ultimate goal (Mrva-Montoya 2020a, 17–18; 2022b, 743). While backlist titles will inevitably require remediation, the cost and effort involved in retrofitting accessibility features underscores the importance of adopting a born-accessible workflow from the start.

As Bill Kasdorf (2018, 17) notes, while ' "born digital" does not guarantee "born accessible" ', the effort required to produce accessible content in digital-first or format-neutral workflow is substantially less than in conventional publishing practices. The American Physical Society demonstrated this potential as early as 2010 by pioneering the use of the DAISY XML format for journal publishing (Gardner et al. 2009). Their experience, along with other early adopters, shows that while the transition to inclusive workflows requires significant initial investment, it ultimately creates more efficient and sustainable publishing processes.

Quality Assurance and Certification

The shift towards inclusive publishing workflows raises a critical question: how can publishers ensure their accessibility efforts are actually effective? While quality control has always been an integral part of the book publishing process, with publishers described as 'the guardians of truth because of [their] rigorous approach to content selection, enhancement and production' (Publishers Association 2019), accessibility introduces new dimensions of complexity that challenge traditional quality assurance approaches.

In the case of print publications, publishers have always been in control of the reader experience by making decisions about the book design and layout, the choice of typefaces, and paper quality. This is different with digital books, particularly with reflowable EPUB files, where the reading experience relies to a great degree on 'the usability of the device and of the specific software used to render the EPUB file on that device' (Sandusky 2012). Accessibility adds further complexity by introducing assistive technologies to the mix as well as the need for discovery and procurement requirements.

Effective accessibility implementation requires a comprehensive, multi-layered testing approach that goes beyond simple technical validation. At the content level, all elements – from main text to image descriptions – must be rigorously evaluated for 'accuracy, clarity and completeness' through an accessibility-focused editorial process. This human review ensures that accessibility features not only exist but genuinely serve their intended purpose. Technical validation forms the next critical layer, with tools like EPUBCheck verifying basic file integrity and specialised accessibility checkers such as Ace by DAISY examining EPUB-specific accessibility features. However, technical validation alone cannot guarantee real-world usability. Publications must also undergo cross-device testing to verify consistent functionality across different reading systems and assistive technologies. Most crucially, direct testing by users with print disability provides essential insights that automated tools and standard review processes cannot capture. As Ganner et al. (2023, 190–92) emphasise, such user testing becomes particularly valuable during the initial implementation of inclusive publishing workflows, when publishers are still developing their understanding of practical accessibility requirements.

The scope and complexity of these testing requirements helps explain publishers' current lack of confidence in their accessibility implementation. A 2020 survey of Australian publishers revealed that none felt 'extremely confident' about the accessibility of their publications, while 50 per cent were only 'somewhat confident'. Even those with improved workflows and guidelines expressed uncertainty about their final outputs, particularly when the production was outsourced (Mrva-Montoya 2020a). The situation appears little changed in 2022, with only 26 per cent of educational publishers reporting that they conducted formal accessibility compliance checks (Mrva-Montoya 2022a, 743). As industry expert Jens Tröger observes, publishers' lack of confidence in their final outputs directly correlates with their lack of trust in their workflows and testing tools.[70]

To address these challenges, the industry has developed various certification approaches. Fondazione LIA, operating since 2014, offers Italian publishers, as well as international players, a file-level conformance-

---

[70] Jens Tröger, personal communication, 14 April 2024.

checking service through their VCC (Verification, Conversion and Certification) platform. Their process combines automated testing with manual verification, resulting in algorithmically generated ONIX 3.0 accessibility characteristics and a certification label for validated ebooks.[71] In contrast, Benetech's Global Certified Accessible (GCA) programme takes a more comprehensive approach, assessing and certifying entire publisher workflows rather than individual files. Certified publishers are granted the GCA certification 'seal of approval' and can include information that the title is certified by Benetech's Global Certified Accessible credential in the EPUB Schema metadata.[72]

However, certification programmes alone may not guarantee industry-wide transformation. Writing in the context of the sustainability movement, Poynton (2017, 29) raises fundamental concerns about certification schemes, arguing they often 'fail to deliver industry-wide transformation, all the while becoming an industry in its own right'. His critique has particular relevance for accessibility certification, where high costs present a significant barrier to adoption. The Benetech certification programme, for instance, costs US$2,400–$9,600 for accreditation and US$1,800–$7,200 for annual certification (August 2024), putting it out of reach for many organisations, especially smaller publishers. Beyond cost barriers, Poynton identifies an 'excessive reliance on "outsiders" and not on local capacity' as a critical weakness (Poynton 2017, 33). Perhaps most troubling is his observation that certification systems have proven ineffective in 'achieving deep, sector-wide transformation', typically reaching 'no more than 10% of any industry in which they operate' (Poynton 2017, 36). These limitations suggest the need to rethink how certification programmes can better serve the goal of industry-wide accessibility implementation.

Poynton's alternative 'Values, Transparency, Transformation and Verification' (VT-TV) model offers valuable insights for accessibility implementation. At its foundation, strong organisational *values* should inform policy and its execution, at every level. *Transparency* serves as

---

[71] Cristina Mussinelli and Elisa Molinari, personal communication, 7 February 2024.

[72] https://bornaccessible.benetech.org/global-certified-accessible/.

a crucial second step, requiring companies to conduct thorough audits of their processes and supply chains to identify accessibility barriers and improvement opportunities. This transparent assessment creates the foundation for meaningful change. The *transformation* stage is described as a journey during which the organisation implements training, develops projects, builds capacity, learns, and innovates. Critical to this stage is the integration of external partners (such as freelancers and ebook-conversion houses in the case of publishing) who must align with the organisation's accessibility commitments. Success depends on robust reporting mechanisms to understand and reflect on progress and inspire change internally and externally. The final *verification* process introduces a paradigm shift from traditional paid certification programmes, which often presents conflict of interest, towards a more dynamic system of local verification by NGOs. This approach, which can be funded through industry memberships, foundations, or government support (Poynton 2017, 39–65), provides more authentic and contextualised feedback on accessibility progress, as demonstrated by the operation of Fondazione LIA.

The contrasting approaches of Benetech and Fondazione LIA illustrate these principles in practice. LIA's localised approach, with tiered membership based on publisher size, has achieved remarkable industry engagement – reaching 80 per cent of Italian trade publishers and 60 per cent of educational publishers. Their platform now hosts over 35,000 accessible ebooks, demonstrating how accessibility certification can scale when adapted to local industry conditions.[73]

While certification systems offer significant advantages – providing clear roadmaps, guidelines, and resources for organisations to follow, while building credibility and confidence in consumers – they must be carefully designed to avoid potential pitfalls. The challenge lies in preventing certification from becoming a mere checkbox exercise that prioritises technical compliance over genuine accessibility and usability. Success requires striking a delicate balance: maintaining rigorous standards while ensuring the system remains practical and adaptable for organisations of varying sizes and capabilities. This balanced approach

---

[73] Cristina Mussinelli and Lisa Molinari, personal communication, 7 February 2024.

ensures that certification drives meaningful accessibility improvements rather than simply creating administrative burden.

Accessible Book Supply Chain

While certification systems provide valuable guidance for accessibility implementation, their success ultimately depends on the broader publishing ecosystem and supply chain. Publishers are key drivers in creating accessible publications, but they must also ensure these books are discoverable and available to people with print disability to address what Harpur and Stein (2021, 194) identify as a critical market failure underpinning the book famine. This challenge plays out across a complex supply chain involving distributors, libraries, hardware manufacturers, and software providers who all mediate access to books.

Within this complex ecosystem, publishers are responsible for the production of accessible books and the creation and distribution of accessibility metadata. This metadata serves as a crucial bridge, enabling readers with print disability to discover suitable content outside specialist libraries while allowing publishers to measure the impact of their accessibility work (eBOUND Canada 2024, 10). However, as Fondazione LIA's 2022 white paper highlights, despite the availability of metadata standards and guidance, information rarely reaches end users due to supply chain participants lacking awareness and technical knowledge of accessibility metadata implementation and visibility (Fondazione LIA 2022).

Recent developments demonstrate both progress and persistent challenges. In July 2023, EDItEUR, a standards organisation, expanded accessibility metadata in ONIX (an XML-based standard for rich book metadata) as part of Codelist 196 values to make them more descriptive (EDItEUR 2023), including information about conformance to standards or certification. Yet adoption remains limited – many metadata management systems don't include the up-to-date Codelist 196 values, and few distributors display them. The technical nature of accessibility metadata creates barriers for both publishers and end users (EDRLab 2022). This is evidenced by the 2022 UK survey, whereby only 38 per cent of respondents included Schema accessibility data with EPUB files, 14 per cent of publishers included accessibility metadata in the ONIX Codelist 196, while 43 per cent of publishers provided no accessibility metadata whatsoever (Alexander 2022, 699; PAAG 2022).

The library sector adds another layer of complexity through its use of MARC21 (MAchine-Readable Cataloguing) Records for bibliographic data (Library of Congress 2009). Despite the 2018 addition of dedicated accessibility fields: 341 Accessibility Content (a machine-readable field that requires controlled vocabulary) and 532 Accessibility Note (a free-text summary of the accessibility features, hazards, and deficiencies of a resource), library adoption remains limited (Accessible Libraries 2023). Organisations such as eBOUND Canada (2024) and the International Federation of Library Associations and Institutions (IFLA) are working to address these challenges through international best practices and guidelines on the recording and use of accessibility metadata. At the same time, W3C's ongoing work on metadata standards (W3C 2024a, 2024b), and user experience guides (W3C 2021) promises to make accessibility information more comprehensible and useful across the supply chain.

The importance of an accessible supply chain has been recognised in legislation like the EAA, which mandates accessibility across products and services, including hardware, operating systems, ebooks, reading software, and ecommerce (25). Even if accessibility metadata is rarely displayed at this stage on mainstream ecommerce sites or in public libraries, it is important that publishers provide this information in preparation for when such displays become the norm. Much of the work required for ecommerce sites to be accessible is tied up with ensuring compliance with web accessibility standards. While global corporations such as Amazon (2022) and Google (n.d.) have been working on ensuring their devices and services accessible, VitalSource and Redshelf, both certified by Benetech as accessible providers of textbooks and other digital learning resources, lead in displaying accessibility metadata to the users.[74]

The library sector, with its established history of accessible service provision (see Wentz et al. 2015) and recognition as an 'authorized entity' under the Marrakesh Treaty, continues to drive innovation through

---

[74] https://get.vitalsource.com/intl/vitalsource-advantage/accessibility.

initiatives like the Canadian Public Library Accessibility Resource Centre,[75] demonstrating the potential for systematic change when stakeholders embrace accessibility as a core value.

While this chapter has demonstrated that successful implementation of inclusive publishing requires systematic transformation across organisational structures, workflows, quality assurance processes, and supply chains, format accessibility represents just one dimension of truly inclusive publishing. The industry's focus on creating born-accessible publications, though crucial, must be accompanied by broader cultural and structural changes aligned with human rights model of disability. The next chapter examines three critical intersections of disability and publishing that demand equal attention: the severe underrepresentation of people with disability in publishing workforce, the limited presence of disabled characters and experiences in published content, and the ongoing challenges around inclusive and accessible language practices in editorial workflows.

---

[75] https://accessiblelibraries.ca/

4 Inclusive Publishing beyond Formats

Inclusive publishing extends far beyond the creation of born-accessible formats, encompassing fundamental questions about whose voices are heard and whose experiences shape the publishing landscape. While technological innovations have expanded access to content, true inclusivity requires addressing the systemic barriers that people with print and other disabilities face throughout the publishing ecosystem. This chapter examines how disability intersects with publishing across three critical domains where change is urgently needed.

First, I will examine the paucity of staff with disability in the publishing industry. Despite increasing awareness of the need for diversity, people with disability remain significantly underrepresented in the industry. This exclusion has far-reaching consequences: it not only denies disabled individuals professional opportunities but also deprives the industry of crucial lived experience and expertise needed to publish authentic disability content.

Second, I will explore the issue of representation of people with disability in literature focusing specifically on children's books. The stories we read shape our understanding of the world, yet, too often, people with disability are either absent from these narratives or depicted in ways that reinforce harmful stereotypes. Addressing this gap is crucial for creating literature that reflects the full diversity of human experience.

Finally, I will discuss the importance of inclusive and accessible language. The representational failures are inextricably linked to language practices within publishing that continue to reflect and reinforce ableist assumptions. Language is a powerful tool in shaping perceptions, and the publishing industry must be mindful of the words it uses and the ways in which content is presented.

While previous chapters focused specifically on print disability, this analysis broadens to consider disability more holistically within the context of diversity and inclusion. Many accessibility features that benefit people with print disability also serve aging populations and non-native speakers, illustrating how inclusive design principles can have wide-reaching benefits. Moreover, the barriers to participation and representation that affect people with print disability often mirror those faced by people with other disabilities and marginalised groups, highlighting the intersectional nature of inequality in the publishing industry.

This chapter argues that meaningful inclusive publishing requires a fundamental transformation of the industry itself as demanded by the human right model of disability. Beyond format accessibility, we must reimagine publishing systems and practices to reflect and serve the full spectrum of human diversity. Only through such comprehensive change can publishing fulfil its potential as a truly inclusive cultural force rather than merely offering accommodations.

Inclusive Workplaces

Publishers have historically acted as gatekeepers of ideas (Coser 1975, 15). According to Nancy Roberts, this traditional role becomes problematic when publishing houses lack staff diversity, as it negatively impacts both how diverse authors are treated and the overall diversity of published works. Yet, as Roberts notes, 'the publishing sector has been slow to react to the increasing importance of diversity and inclusion' (Roberts 2021, 260). This institutional inertia has created a persistent barrier to innovation, especially in accessibility initiatives. Without employees with disabilities – including those with print disability – publishers are missing out on diverse perspectives, better understanding of the needs and preferences of people with print disability, and their expertise in assistive technologies. As a disability-rights lawyer Haben Girma compellingly argues, 'Employees with disabilities drive innovation. Disability creates a constraint, and embracing constraints spurs inventive solutions' (2017).

The transformative potential of including disabled perspectives is powerfully demonstrated in adjacent cultural sectors, particularly theatre and performance studies (see Hadley 2022) and the gallery and museum sector. Rieger and colleagues document how the codesign process not only created an accessible and inclusive exhibition, but fundamentally shifted institutional culture from superficial and surface-level accommodations towards genuine inclusion where access is seen 'as central to curatorial methodology' (Rieger et al. 2023, 182–83). Similarly, Georgina Kleege's insights on art accessibility reveal the deeper implications of inclusive design:

> the ultimate goal is not merely to explain visual art to blind people in the hope that this cultural access will compensate for the loss of sight. Rather, the hope is that blind people can bring a perspective that has not been articulated before ... The integration of blind perceptions and experiences will change the foundational assumptions of the culture; change how the human condition is defined. (Kleege 2018, 13)

This transformative potential remains largely untapped in publishing, where the inclusion of people with print disability in developing books, textbooks, and platforms could revolutionise not just accessibility implementation but the fundamental nature of reading and knowledge dissemination.

Much of the discourse around diversity and inclusion in Australia, Canada, the UK, and the United States has centred on race, gender, and sexual orientation diversity, in the context of publishing industries that are overwhelmingly white, female, heterosexual, and middle class. While this focus has intensified in response to 'the historical, cultural, and legal developments in the latter part of the twentieth century' (Calvard 2021, 1), and gained particular momentum following the Black Lives Matter movement of 2020, disability representation remains notably absent from many of these conversations. This gap between different aspects of diversity efforts highlights the need for a more comprehensive approach to inclusion that addresses intersecting forms of marginalisation within publishing.

This gap between diversity efforts and disability representation has deep consequences for the publishing industry's approach to accessibility. As Kenny Fries (2018) writes, 'disability is too often excluded in discussions of diversity, a good deal of which, for good reason, focuses on race. This silence is especially noteworthy because disability crosses racial, gender, sexuality, class, and national boundaries. This lack of discussion, and inclusion, of disability is reflected in publishing'. When publishing workplaces lack employees with print disability, they miss crucial lived experience that could inform accessibility initiatives at every stage of production. The scale of this representational crisis remains difficult to quantify – notably in the context of this book, there exists no specific data on employment rates of people with print disability in publishing, with available statistics only capturing broad categories of disability and long-term health conditions combined. This absence of granular data itself reflects the industry's limited engagement with disability as a vital aspect of workplace diversity.

The industry surveys also fail to capture the complex reality of intersectional identities. The concept of intersectionality, first coined by Kimberlé Crenshaw (1989) to refer to the specific oppression black women face on account of being black and female, is particularly relevant to inclusive publishing as it brings attention to how disability intersects with other aspects of identity such as race, gender, sexuality, and class. To paraphrase Crenshaw, the intersectional experience is greater than the sum of disability and other forms of discrimination, creating unique barriers and challenges that demand nuanced understanding. Alice Wong, for example, powerfully illustrates how different aspects of identity can compound the challenges of working in the publishing industry. As a disabled person of colour, she has faced systemic racism and disability discrimination as intertwined problems (Wong 2023). Dutch YA writer and activist Marieke Nijkamp, who is autistic, non-binary and queer, has also spoken about their experiences of marginalisation, noting that their voice was 'seen as less important than that of a neurotypical person' (Haller 2024, 151).

Yet these vital intersectional experiences remain obscured in industry surveys that persist in employing a single-axis approach to discrimination. Blackham et al. (2023, 40) acknowledge that while 'intersectionality offers important ideas to advance and extend understandings of inequality, it can be difficult to operationalise in practice'. This methodological challenge represents a critical blind spot in the industry's efforts to understand and address workplace diversity.

Industry surveys provide crucial baseline data for understanding representation gaps, though their current structure often fails to capture the nuanced reality of disability in publishing workplaces. The following data reveal not only current representation levels but also highlights specific areas where the industry needs to improve to create genuinely inclusive workplaces.

The first Diversity Baseline Survey of publishing houses and review journals was conducted in 2015 by Lee & Low Books, the largest multicultural children's book publisher in the United States. Only 7.6 per cent of respondents reported having a disability. Designers (18 per cent) and book reviewers (12 per cent) showed higher representation of disability than the industry average, likely due to the higher prevalence of freelancing opportunities that enable working from home – a crucial accessibility factor for people with limited mobility (Lee & Bow Books 2016). In the 2019 survey, 11 per cent of staff and 22 per cent of interns self-reported a disability with mental illness (45 per cent), physical disability (22 per cent), and chronic illness (20 per cent) comprising the majority. The higher diversity among interns suggested a promising trend, contingent on these individuals remaining in the workforce (Lee & Bow Books 2020). By 2023, disability representation had increased to 16.2 per cent of respondents identified as being disabled, with significant growth across all departments: 'Marketing & Publicity rose from 10% to 20%; Editorial from 12% to 18.9%; Reviewers from 19% to 26.2%; and Interns from 22% to 27.6%', potentially reflecting the wider adoption of remote and hybrid work (Lee & Bow Books 2024).

Canadian publishing has shown similar trends. The Association of Canadian Publishers' 2018 survey of reported almost 17 per cent of respondents having a disability (2019, 2), rising substantially to 26 per cent in the 2022. This increase has been attributed to the long-term impact of COVID-19 and a decrease in stigma around chronic illness, neurodiversities, and mental health issues (Association of Canadian Publishers 2023, 10, 24).

In the UK, disability representation in publishing has grown steadily, from 2 per cent in 2017 to 6.6 per cent in 2019 (Publishers Association 2020, 59) and 8 per cent in 2020 (Publishers Association 2021, 20), reaching 13 per cent reported having a disability or long-term health condition in 2021, with mental illness accounting for almost half. Yet these figures remain well below the broader UK's working-age population, where 20 per cent people report disability and 33 per cent indicate long-term health condition (Publishers Association 2022, 25–26). By 2022, the figure rose to 16 per cent (Publishers Association 2023).

The UK Publishers Association responded in 2023 with an 'Inclusivity Action Plan' outlining ten commitments for 2023–2026. This comprehensive initiative mandates senior leadership-driven policies, accountability frameworks, data collection and industry-wide standards, staff inclusivity training, flexible working options, clear paths for career progression, mentoring for underrepresented groups, targeted hiring, pay equity and salary transparency, and notably, ensuring 'output is accessible, authentic and inclusive including content, design, imagery and language' (Publisher Association, n.d.).

Australia's first Publishing Industry Workforce Survey on Diversity and Inclusion in 2022 revealed that while 24.7 per cent of publishing professionals reported living with a disability or long-term physical or mental health condition, only 5.2 per cent of respondents explicitly identified as disabled (Driscoll & Bowen 2023, 318). Similarly to the UK, this number is much lower than the estimation by the Australian Disability Network (n.d.) that 17.8 per cent of females and 17.6 per cent of males in Australia live with disability. In response to the findings, the Australian Publishers Association (APA) established a Diversity & Inclusion Working Group and in January 2024 launched the Diversity and Inclusion Plan 2024–25, which, in addition to improving diversity of the workforce, aims to focus on 'disability and neurodiversity', and 'inclusive publishing formats and accessible content' (APA 2024).

Crucially, none of these surveys identify the percentage of employees with print disability specifically, which is likely to be much smaller. One of those is Stacy Scott, Head of Accessibility at Taylor & Francis, and the Chair of the Publishing Accessibility Action Group (PAAG) in the UK. Another is Simon Holt, Accessible Publishing and Disability Inclusion Champion at Elsevier, also based in the UK. Holt and colleagues advocate for more detailed disability data collection and understanding of required workplace adjustments to enhance inclusion in scholarly publishing (Holt et al. 2023). Future industry surveys, however, must also seek data about intersectional inequalities to drive meaningful, sustainable improvements in workforce diversity.

While industry surveys reveal important trends in disability representation, transforming publishing workplaces into truly accessible spaces requires concrete action and structural change. In order to open the publishing industry to people with print and other disabilities, workplaces themselves need to be accessible. The Inklusion Guide, launched in the UK in 2022, represents a significant step forward by providing best-practice accessibility provisions to help organisations deliver inclusive online and face-to-face events, alongside practical advice on hiring disabled staff. The guide establishes clear requirements for companies: accommodating any access needs, providing flexible working and working from home options, appointing dedicated access officers, implementing disability and accessibility training for all staff, and engaging access consultants (Carpenter 2022; Inklusion Guide 2022, 88).

Within the scholarly publishing sector specifically, the Coalition for Diversity and Inclusion in Scholarly Communications has advanced this work through their C4DISC Toolkit for Disability Equity in Scholarly Communications. This resource equips both employees and employers with guidance on flexible working arrangement and workplace adjustments, fostering inclusive conversations around disability at work, and ensuring supportive hiring and induction processes (C4DISC 2023).

Representations of Disability

While creating accessible and inclusive workplaces is crucial, equally important is ensuring that published content itself reflects and speaks to diverse experiences. It is critical that people with print disability not only have access to books but also encounter representation of themselves in stories and published content. Arguably the most common genre written by people with disability are memoirs and autobiographical works. As Thomas Couser notes, personal narratives about disability have grown increasingly prominent since the 1990, emerging alongside and amplifying the disability rights movement. Through these accounts, writers are simultaneously sharing their lived experiences with readers and reclaiming agency over how disability is portrayed in literature (Couser 2003, 2018). Matthew Rubery's (2022) discussion of dyslexia memoirs provides a particularly insightful illustration on how valuable personal testimony has been to developing understanding of what it means to experience dyslexia and how it shapes one's interaction with printed text.

While personal narratives have carved out crucial space for authentic disability representation, the broader literary landscape remains complex and often problematic. Many historical works by disabled authors remain disconnected from their creators' lived experiences. Take Australian literature, where deafness profoundly shaped the writing of celebrated authors Henry Lawson and Judith Wright, as scholars Amanda Tink and Jessica White have demonstrated. Yet most readers encounter their works without any awareness of this fundamental aspect of their creative lives. This systematic overlooking of disability in literary history reinforces harmful assumptions about who can create literature. As Tink and White argue, 'This creates the impression writing is something disabled people can't do' – perpetuating a self-defeating cycle where disabled writers remain invisible even as their works endure.[76]

This invisibility extends beyond individual authors to shape broader cultural attitudes about disability literature. As Kenny Fries observes, 'Writing by disabled writers has often [been] seen more as "therapy" than art. Disabled protagonists are not seen as universal, despite the fact that all of us, at one time or another in our lives, will be, either temporarily or permanently, disabled' (Fries 2018). While Fries highlights these reductive attitudes, the literary significance of disability writing transcends such narrow categorisation. This tension between authentic representation and literary reception is further illuminated by Claire Barker and Stuart Murray, who argue that the 'literary representations of disability, whether realist or non-realist, social/political or fantastical, open up our understanding of the multiplicities inherent within disability experiences' (Barker & Murray 2018, 11).

As Barker and Murray further demonstrate, 'Disability is everywhere in literature', though it rarely stands independently in the narrative. Instead, it is typically conceptualised within complex cultural and social contexts,

---

[76] Tink and White 2023. See also 'Writing Disability in Australia', a project that highlights disabled writers and disability-focused literature: www.austlit.edu.au/writingdisability.

intersecting with fundamental questions about what defines humanity while simultaneously triggering opposing societal reactions that frame disabled individuals as either 'deviant' or 'special'. The concept of disability also tends to evoke powerful emotional responses including shock, fear, and pity, while serving as a focus for spiritual and philosophical contemplation. Crucially, they argue that 'disability is made to work primarily as a metaphor, a textual device that, precisely because of the ways in which it reconfigures what disability means, ultimately has little to say about the actual lives experienced by those with disabilities' (Barker & Murray 2018, 1–2).

The literary reduction of disability to metaphor becomes particularly evident in genre fiction, where specific disability tropes have become codified into the storytelling framework itself. In fact, genre fiction commonly features recurring representations of disability that serve as recognisable motifs or 'icons' within specific genre contexts. These disability representations aren't random but rather carry particular emotional and symbolic weight, functioning as established literary devices that align with and reinforce familiar narrative patterns and genre conventions (Cheyne 2019, 7). Horror stories, for example, often fall into a problematic pattern when portraying disabled characters, typically casting them in one of two extreme roles: either as threatening villains or as helpless victims. Romance novel readers might expect a common but problematic story arc: a character with a disability will somehow be 'healed' or 'cured' as part of their journey to romantic fulfilment. This trope suggests that disability is incompatible with love and happiness. Yet, as Madison Nankervis argues, 'Everyone deserves to see themselves written in the pages of the book, they deserve to see that they get a happy ending, that they get love. Increasing diversity in romance novels is a necessity, not an option' (Nankervis 2022, 361).

Nankervis also highlights the persistent lack of neurodivergence and disability representation in romance novels, while acknowledging pioneering authors such as Helen Hoang and Talia Hibbert who are leading crucial change. Significantly, she notes that the self-publishing industry has proven far more successful at producing diverse content than traditional publishing houses (Nankervis 2022, 361).

The challenges of representation in genre fiction mirror equally significant gaps in children's literature, where authentic disability representation could have profound developmental impact. The results of a qualitative study involving 475 students in a public elementary school in the United States, published in 2014, show that 'Through exploring characters in books, children not only learned about various disabilities, but they came to understand characters with disabilities as full and complex beings, similar in many ways to themselves' (Adomat 2014). This is consistent with findings from studies on human brain development and healthy cognitive function, which shows that increasing children's exposure to diversity at an early stage is crucial, as children aged 3–5 years old already show 'preferences based on what is most familiar to them, and discriminatory behaviour is influenced by biased perception' (Penrose 2023, 171).

A positive impact is possible only if a disability-related theme is present in a book in the first place and it is presented in an inclusive way, which is not always the case. Findings from a 2010 review of 100 children's books featuring disability available to schoolchildren in the UK suggested that while there were 'some good examples of inclusive literature "out there", discriminatory language and/or negative stereotypes about disability continue[d] to be present in a range of more contemporary children's books' (Beckett et al. 2010, 373).

In 2016, Linda Gilmore and Glenn Howard published a review of fifty children's books that tackle individual differences and disabilities. They concluded that 'each book has the potential to increase awareness, knowledge, understanding and acceptance of those who are different'. However, they noted 'a very limited empirical base to demonstrate the effectiveness of children's books for promoting awareness, knowledge, understanding and acceptance of diversity' (Gilmore & Howard 2016, 243).

The disconnect between potential impact and actual representation remains stark. Despite the potential to affirm the identity and experiences of disabled children and foster a culture of inclusion, empathy, and respect, the US-based Cooperative Children's Book Center's 2019 study found that only 3.4 per cent of children's books featured main characters with disability (CCBC 2020). This number grew modestly to 4 per cent in the 2022 study of books, with main characters having a range of 'physical, cognitive, neurological, and psychiatric' disabilities, while 6 per cent of books were classified as being as 'about' disability (CCBC 2023a), where 'the main character/

subject or a significant secondary character is disabled or the subject of the book is about disabilities or the disability experiences' (CCBC 2023b). To give these numbers context, the Pew Research reported that in the 2021–2022 school year, disabled students made up 15 per cent of national public school enrolment in the United States (Gilmore & Howard 2016, 245), while up to 27 per cent of Americans reported some type of a disability in 2023, including 4.8 per cent of US adults who have a vision disability (Center for Disease Control and Prevention 2023).

These stark statistics reflect deeper systemic issues within the publishing industry. In her analysis of disability representation in children's books, Margaret Kingsbury (2021) identifies persistent barriers that disabled writers and illustrators face when seeking publication. These barriers include widespread prejudice against disabled characters and their creators, where individuals with disability are portrayed as pitiable, superhuman, evil, burdens, or objects of inspiration, rather than as fully realised individuals. The challenges are even greater for authors and characters with intersecting marginalised identities. Kingsbury further emphasises that the publishing process itself, including industry events, remain largely inaccessible to disabled creators.

Kingsbury links the marked increase in interest in books with disabled main characters since the Black Lives Matter movement to the greater interest in diversity in general. As she writes, 'Uplifting marginalized voices for one group does help to uplift other marginalized voices, though specifically addressing some of the unique problems groups of people face is also important' (Kingsbury 2021).

To improve the representation of disabled narratives, Kingsbury calls for publishers to employ more people with disability and publish more books by disabled creators. To do so, publishers need to make sure their workplaces, publishing workflows, and events are accessible, and provide staff training on ableism and disability. In terms of content, Kingsbury calls for publishers to 'publish more books with disabled characters that aren't "about" disability', hire sensitivity readers to avoid reproducing stereotypes, and work with disability organisations (Kingsbury 2021). For example, Alice Wong, founder and director of the US-based Disability Visibility Project, an online community focused on producing, distributing, and amplifying disability media and culture, has edited and written books showcasing first-person accounts of the modern disability experience, which were published by Penguin Random House (e.g. Wong 2020, 2022, 2024). Nevertheless, such books remain rare in the list of large publishers.

While major publishers have been slow to change, individuals and organisations operating outside mainstream publishing have stepped in to improve the representation of diverse voices. As Penrose notes, 'more children's books on disabilities are being self-published by authors who have personal experience with or connection to the disability' (Penrose 2023, 174). For example, in 2023, Vision Australia released a series of Big Visions books. In addition to featuring individuals living with blindness – Matt Formston (a professional surfer), Craig Shanahan (a chef and cafe owner), and Nikki Hind (a fashion designer) – each book contains braille alongside printed text.[77] While these books are aimed particularly at children with low or no vision, the fact that they were published in collaboration with a small press, Berbay Publishing, and are distributed by Simon and Schuster, indicates a goal of reaching a wider audience and prompting conversations about the different ways of reading.

All publishers need to pay attention to how characters with disability are presented. They should not be used as inspiration for non-disabled people in what Stella Young described as 'inspiration porn' in her TEDxSydney talk in 2014 (Young 2014; Penrose 2023, 174). Similarly, Haben Girma advocates for creating positive disability stories by focusing on the perspective of the disabled person, avoiding assumptions, and moving beyond the inspiration cliché when writing about disabled individuals (Girma 2016).

The Power of Words

While initiatives like Vision Australia's Big Visions series demonstrate progress in representation and physical accessibility through braille inclusion, the publishing industry must also grapple with fundamental questions of language use. It must navigate two distinct, but interconnected, imperatives: creating inclusive content that authentically represents diverse perspectives, and ensuring that content remains accessible to readers of all abilities.

---

[77] https://shop.visionaustralia.org/campaigns/big-visions-books.html.

Ideally, books and other publishing outputs should be both inclusive and accessible, recognising the importance of acknowledging and representing diverse perspectives and making sure the content is usable by as many people as possible. These are two different imperatives. According to the Linguistic Society of America (2016), 'Inclusive language acknowledges diversity, conveys respect to all people, is sensitive to differences, and promotes equal opportunities.' This speaks to representation and dignity. In contrast, accessible language is about being 'Able to be (readily) understood or appreciated' (*Oxford English Dictionary*). It is about writing content in a way that allows users, regardless of ability and circumstance, to get the information they need, sometimes requiring simplified versions of content to be produced. While a text might perfectly represent diverse perspectives, it fails if readers cannot engage with its content. Conversely, perfectly accessible writing falls short if it perpetuates exclusionary viewpoints or erases marginalised voices.

The publishing industry must therefore embrace a dual commitment: crafting content that both honours human diversity and ensures reading equity. This requires careful attention to both what we say and how we say it, recognising that words hold the power to both include and exclude, to illuminate and to obscure. The future of publishing lies in mastering this delicate balance.

The disability rights movement that emerged in 1960s America fundamentally transformed how society discusses and conceptualises disability. Alongside other minority groups, disability activists fought for equal treatment, access, and opportunity, recognising that lasting change required dismantling both institutional barriers and entrenched societal attitudes (ADL 2017). Their efforts sparked extensive academic research examining disability terminology, media representation, and technological access, creating a rich framework that powerfully informs modern media practices, including publishing (e.g. Riley II 2012; Ellis & Goggin 2015; Ellis et al. 2019).

Contemporary publishers face critical decisions about disability language that reflect deeper societal and cultural tensions. At the heart of this discourse lies the distinction between person-first versus identity-first approach. The person-first approach ('people with print disability') focuses on people rather than on their medical condition(s). In contrast, identity-first or disability-first language ('print-disabled people') positions disability as an identity category and signifies belonging to a cultural group (PWDA 2021, 6). The person-first approach, enshrined in the US Disabilities Act (1990), marked a revolutionary shift by emphasising individual humanity over medical conditions. It was seen as a significant step in the disability rights movement as it helped 'create a message about people with disabilities that contrasted with narrow stereotypes and misleading myths of the past' (Haller et al. 2006, 66).

Yet language evolves with cultural understanding. The disability rights community has increasingly embraced identity-first language, aligned with the social model of disability that located disability 'not an innate characteristic of the individual, but rather it is societal attitudes and structures that make people disabled'. Identity-first language acknowledges disability as an integral part of a person, without any derogatory connotations, diverging from the perspective that frames it as a medical issue in need of a cure. Instead, it 'recognizes disability as a culture, promoting autonomy, agency, and choice over one's destiny' (Best et al. 2022, 127). This shift reflects a broader movement towards disability pride and self-determination, challenging publishers to thoughtfully navigate these evolving linguistic preferences while respecting the diverse perspectives within disability communities.

The landscape of disability language in Australia reflects a nuanced interplay between institutional practice and personal identity. Government bodies and advocacy organisations like People with Disability Australia (PWDA) typically embrace person-first language, while many individuals within disability communities prefer identity-first terminology. This divergence highlights how language choices carry deep personal and political significance.

The fundamental principle, as Joanne Arciuli and Tom Shakespeare (2023, 20) compellingly argue, is to: 'call people what they want to be called'. This deceptively simple directive demands careful attention to individual preferences while avoiding problematic euphemisms such as 'differently abled', which can turn into dysphemism. For example, the term 'special needs', once intended as a respectful alternative, now carries negative connotations that demonstrate how language evolves with cultural understanding. Similarly, the word 'cripple' has undergone a remarkable transformation, reclaimed by some within disability communities as what Haller et al. (2006, 65) describe as 'a source of militant pride'.

These linguistic complexities deepen when considering intersectional identities and cultural variations. Language preferences shift not only across English-speaking countries (Arciuli & Shakespeare 2023, 20, 23), but also within distinct cultural communities. The Deaf community offers a powerful example, as explored by Ladd (2003), where language choices intertwine with cultural identity in ways that may differ significantly from other disability communities. This intersection of disability, culture, and identity creates a rich tapestry of language preferences that defies one-size-fits-all solutions. Publishers must therefore approach language choices with both cultural awareness and individual sensitivity, recognising that respectful communication requires ongoing dialogue with diverse disability communities.

The impact of disability language extends far beyond direct references to individuals, penetrating deep into our everyday metaphors and expressions. Liat Ben-Moshe powerfully articulates how seemingly casual uses of terms like 'retarded', 'lame', or 'blind' perpetuate disability stigma, even when applied to abstract concepts: 'By using a label, which is commonly associated with disabled people to denote deficiency, a lack, or an ill-conceived notion, we reproduce the oppression of people with disabilities' (Ben-Moshe 2005, 108–109). This observation reveals how language shapes societal attitudes through subtle, but pervasive, patterns of association.

Similar concerns arise with medical terminology that reinforces a 'sick role' narrative. Phrases like 'suffering from' or 'wheelchair-bound' position disability as inherently negative, while alternatives like 'living with' a condition or 'wheelchair user' acknowledge agency and normalise disability as one aspect of human experience (Haller et al. 2006, 66). These linguistic choices reflect broader shifts in how society conceptualises disability identity and autonomy.

The publishing industry has responded to these evolving understandings through resources like Renée Otmar's *Editing for Sensitivity, Diversity and Inclusion* (2023) and comprehensive guidelines.[78] These tools reflect growing recognition that inclusive language requires intentional, informed choices.

---

[78] See for example C4DISC 2022, Ashwell et al. 2023 and 'ACS Inclusivity Style Guide', www.acs.org/about/diversity/inclusivity-style-guide.html#general-guidelines.

Arciuli and Shakespeare capture the transformative potential of thoughtful language use:

> Terminology is often the frontline of efforts to promote acceptance, and the boundaries of what is acceptable, what is hurtful, what is radical, and what is shameful change fast . . . Having disabled people as professionals; as academics; as journalists; as broadcasters; as comedians can only help, normalizing disability and difference as another dimension to the complexities and fascinations of life. (Arciuli & Shakespeare 2023, 26–27)

Their vision suggests how language can either reinforce barriers or help create a society where disability becomes 'an unremarkable and unremarked-on part of someone's multifaceted identity'.

Books hold unique power to shape cultural narratives through their ability to educate, preserve culture, inspire creativity, foster empathy, and provide entertainment. This power carries profound responsibility: the language choices made in publishing ripple outward, influencing how society perceives, discusses, and values disability. Inclusive language thus becomes not merely a matter of editorial preference but a crucial tool for advancing social justice and human dignity.

While ensuring universal accessibility of a single book across diverse disabilities and literacy levels presents inherent challenges, as books naturally target different audiences, publishers can significantly enhance content accessibility through thoughtful language choices. Ganner et al. (2023, 58) advocate for 'descriptive, multisensory language instead of purely visual expressions', and avoiding reliance purely on colour or spatial description when referring to the location of elements on the page, such as figures. This is particularly important in educational materials and children's books (Ganner et al. 2023, 58).

Publishers may also consider creating 'high interest low reading level' (high-low or hi-lo) or Easy Read versions of books. These adaptations maintain age-appropriate content while employing simpler vocabulary and syntax, serving not only struggling or reluctant readers but also individuals with cognitive and learning disabilities. Content written in Easy Read differs from plain language. Easy Read emphasises simplicity, and is usually accompanied by images and represented in large font size, while plain language focuses on clarity within standard formatting parameters (Australian Government 2020).

For scholarly works, accessibility initiatives have evolved beyond focusing on formats. Plain Language Summaries (PLS) and Taylor & Francis' pioneering Plain Language Summaries of Publications (PLSP) represent significant advances in making complex research accessible to broader audiences.[79] These peer-reviewed, open-access materials align with WCAG 2.1 guidelines requiring clear, simple content presentation or appropriate supplemental materials (W3C WAI 2023). As Rosenberg et al. (2023, 109) argue, these innovations advance 'diversity, equity, inclusion and accessibility in scholarly publishing' by breaking down barriers between academic knowledge and public understanding. Through such adaptations, publishers demonstrate how thoughtful language choices can expand access while maintaining content integrity across diverse audiences.

The publishing industry's journey towards inclusivity extends far beyond the technical challenge of creating accessible formats. Through examination of workplace diversity, literary representation, and evolving language practices, this chapter argues for the need to reimagine fundamental aspects of how books are created and who creates them. Meaningful progress requires fundamental changes to industry structures and practices, rather than surface-level accommodations, to create a publishing landscape that genuinely reflects and serves the full spectrum of human diversity.

---

[79] https://authorservices.taylorandfrancis.com/publishing-your-research/writing-your-paper/how-to-write-a-plain-language-summary/.

From Book Famine to Reading Equity

The transition from book famine to reading equity represents a fundamental transformation in how the publishing industry approaches accessibility. This transformation challenges traditional publishing models while offering unprecedented opportunities for creating truly inclusive access to reading. The publishing industry has been dealing with many major disruptions – from the digital transformation to changing reading habits, increased competition from other media, the rise of self-publishing, growing demand for more diverse and inclusive representation in books, and more recently the impact of artificial intelligence and machine learning on content creation, marketing, and distribution. While ensuring compliance with legal requirements and regulations associated with accessibility has added another layer of complexity to an already challenging environment, these disruptions also represent a time of great opportunity. These industry-wide changes have highlighted the persistent gap between modern publishing capabilities and long-standing accessibility practices.

The historical division where disability agencies, not publishers, were responsible for creating accessible formats continues to shape current industry practices. Industry surveys conducted in 2020–2022 revealed significant barriers to transformation: lack of accessibility awareness and knowledge, limited capacity, staffing constraints, cost, and copyright concerns. These challenges are compounded by the systemic underrepresentation of disability perspectives within publishing – from the paucity of publishing staff with lived experience of disability to the shortage of books written by disabled authors and about disabled characters. Publishers, still operating in largely print-centric environments and struggling with digital workflows, face additional complexity in accommodating the diverse and sometimes conflicting reading needs and format requirements of people with print disability.

But with the introduction of the EAA, publishers can no longer consider only the needs of people who can interact with content traditionally, and relegate the production of accessible formats for people with print disability to alternative-format providers and disability organisations. However, focusing primarily on compliance with accessibility regulations is a restrictive approach that overlooks the broader value proposition of inclusive publishing. The business case for accessibility extends far beyond mitigating legal risks – it encompasses fostering a positive brand image, demonstrating a commitment to inclusivity, and implementing socially responsible and ethical practices. As Manis and Alexander argue, 'By creating quality, accessible content from the inception of the publishing process, publishers will save time, reduce retrospective conversion costs, and address customer needs' (Manis & Alexander 2018, 65). Moreover, the adoption of accessibility standards and inclusive publishing practices has stimulated technological innovation and advancements in the publishing industry, resulting in well-structured digital files that enhance the reading experience for all users, not just those with print disability. By embracing inclusive publishing, publishers can reach a broader audience, increase their readership base, and contribute to a more equitable society. The business case is clear and strong.

The progress towards reading equity has been driven by collaborative efforts across the ecosystem – including alternative-format producers, disability organisations, libraries, publishers, and software developers, who have worked together on standards and guidelines, sharing knowledge, and best practice. Such collaboration with disability agencies helps bridge the accessibility knowledge gap and build industry capacity. Apart from the broad cross-sector initiatives, individual publishers have been collaborating directly with disability and other organisations in the implementation of accessibility policies, inclusive publishing workflows, getting access to the in-depth knowledge of accessibility and the needs, technological capabilities, and requirements of individuals with print disability. These collaborations are essential to ensure reading equity and access to specialised formats.

The path to reading equity requires publishers to focus on creating and disseminating content in ways that serve the broadest possible range of readers. Content should be published in multiple formats, with digital files capable of being read using mainstream devices or specialist assistive technology, and designed in a way to minimise the difficulties of adaptation for alternative formats (such as braille or large print). Some accessibility considerations should also be integrated into the design and production of print materials (such as the use of colour-blindness-friendly palettes), to create a more inclusive and accessible reading experience for a wider audience.

Digital technologies have made the production of born-accessible books possible and remain a key driver in improving access to content for people with print disability, with new hardware and software increasingly built following the principles of inclusive design. However, unlike web accessibility, much of the technology involved in the production, distribution, and usage of ebooks is beyond publishers' control. As Arthur Thompson and Martin Klopstock (2023) of Kogan Page observe, 'accessible ebooks are only as accessible as the platform they are paired with. If an ereader is not compliant with the latest web standards, the user experience and accessibility of the ebook will be compromised'. Recognising this ecosystem complexity and interdependence, the EAA requires not only ebooks but also ereaders and ecommerce platforms to be accessible.

While no format can be universally accessible, reflowable EPUB3 offers the greatest potential for accessibility and caters for the audience with the widest range of needs. As such, much of the focus has been on compliance with web and EPUB accessibility standards. Yet while these technological considerations are important, publishers need to think about the broader context of reading, and how books are read in different geographical, social, technological, or cultural environments. For example, even though readers can resize the text in reflowable EPUB3, which theoretically should make large-print format books redundant, in practice, not all readers with low vision have access to ereading technologies, know how to use them (a case of 'instrumental failure'), or want to use them. Moreover, braille remains an important format as it provides readers who are blind and visually impaired with direct access to literacy and education. Unlike audio formats, braille allows for active engagement with text, supporting skills such as spelling, grammar, and punctuation. Therefore, while born-accessible EPUB3 represents significant progress in accessibility, publishers must maintain support for multiple format options to ensure genuine inclusivity and meet diverse reading preferences and needs.

As technology advances, and new devices, operating systems, and software are introduced, accessibility standards and guidelines will need to adapt. Publishers must stay abreast of developments in these areas and ensure their workflows follow the new requirements, and that front- and backlist publications remain compatible with mainstream and assistive technologies. This does not need to be challenging – many of the new versions are backwards compatible, and keeping on top of developments will ensure a straightforward transition whenever needed. Publishers also need to monitor emerging technologies, which provide new opportunities to enhance and simplify accessibility implementation. For example, advancements in AI, machine learning and natural language processing have improved speech-recognition software and enabled more accurate transcription services. AI can already be used to assist with the automation of some aspects of accessibility implementation, such as content classification, the creation of alternative text for images, and simplified summaries of complex content, but only as part of a process that involves human oversight.

The implementation of inclusive publishing practices varies significantly across the industry. It is clear that bigger publishers in the educational and scholarly sector have made tremendous progress on accessibility implementation. As they have greater resources and a stronger legal and moral imperative, this is not surprising. Having larger publishers onboard is a positive development as their sizeable publishing programmes substantially contribute to achieving reading equity. Some trade publishers and smaller publishers have also been making significant strides towards inclusive publishing, but many are yet to start. As can be seen in the case of the Canadian industry, the availability of government funding is an important factor in supporting accessibility implementation across publishers of all sizes. No doubt, the inadequate support for accessibility considerations in key publishing software, such as Adobe InDesign, contributes towards the cost and difficulty of adopting inclusive publishing practices.

Looking ahead, several research priorities emerge for supporting the transition to reading equity. As the publishing industry undergoes this fundamental transformation, there is a critical need to understand both the macro-level policy impacts and micro-level organisational changes that will shape the future of born-accessible publishing. These research priorities span multiple dimensions: from evaluating the effectiveness of legislative frameworks and their global implementation, to understanding organisational approaches to accessibility implementation, measuring progress towards reading equity, and ensuring the industry itself becomes more inclusive of people with print disabilities.

On the macro level, it will be interesting to see the progress made in accessibility implementation in the European Union over the next few years. While the presence of a major legal framework is an important factor in the move to inclusive publishing, it does not guarantee that publishers will make progress. How the EAA is implemented and how compliance is managed will be important to track from a research perspective. It will also be important to compare the legal and policy landscape surrounding accessibility implementation in the European Union with that of other countries around the world, to evaluate the effectiveness of the enacted measures and to identify areas for improvement. Moreover, there is a need to investigate the progress of accessibility implementation in the Global South, where the book famine has been even more severe, and where there are significant barriers related to the lack of language support in assistive technologies and limited technology and staffing resources (DAISY Consortium n.d.c.).

On the micro, organisational level, more research is needed to understand how publishers are (a) approaching the implementation process from the business perspective, (b) striking the balance between social, legal, or financial considerations, and (c) approaching continuous improvement in accessibility, in view of evolving technologies and reader needs. Better understanding of the costs, benefits, and economic implications of the implementation of inclusive practices will assist accessibility leaders in refining the process, and will help those lagging behind to get started. The need for a certification system and its efficacy in the context of accessibility implementation in the publishing industry also require further research.

More industry surveys are needed to assess the effectiveness of inclusive publishing strategies and their impact on audience reach and engagement. We actually do not know the current extent of the book famine, and how far we are from making reading equity a realised dream. In addition to needing benchmark data, in-depth user-experience studies of individuals with print disability would also be valuable, to gather insights into their preferences, challenges, and needs, in order to inform further development of inclusive publishing practices.

As part of broader inclusivity and diversity strategies, and in line with the human rights model of disability and Article 30 of CRPD, we also need to keep track of the progress in making the publishing industry inclusive of people with print and other disabilities, as staff, authors, and characters in books. As Holt noted, there is a need for clear criteria, measurements, and standards to be developed to successfully benchmark and measure progress in inclusion and diversity initiatives (Holt et al. 2023, 35). There is also a need to capture intersectionality in industry surveys.

The Final Report of the Royal Commission into Violence, Abuse, Neglect and Exploitation of People with Disability in Australia envisions 'a future where people with and without disability live, learn, work, play, create and engage together in safe and diverse communities' (Commonwealth of Australia 2023). This vision aligns perfectly with the goals of inclusive publishing, suggesting that true reading equity goes beyond format accessibility to encompass full participation in the creation and consumption of books. As the publishing industry continues its transformation from addressing the book famine to achieving reading equity, this vision of complete inclusion should guide our collective efforts towards a future where books and the publishing industry are truly accessible to all.

References

Primary sources

Berne Convention for the Protection of Literary and Artistic Works, opened for signature 9 September 1886, 1161 UNTS 30, entered into force 5 December 1887. www.wipo.int/treaties/en/ip/berne/.

The Chafee Amendment, 17 U.S.C. Section 121. 1996 (USA). www.copyright.gov/title17/92chap1.html.

Convention on the Rights of Persons with Disabilities (UN CRPD). United Nations, adopted on 13 December 2006, opened for signature on 30 March 2007, entered into force on 3 May 2008. www.un.org/development/desa/disabilities/convention-on-the-rights-of-persons-with-disabilities.html.

Copyright Amendment (Disability Access and Other Measures) Bill 2017 (Australia). https://parlinfo.aph.gov.au/parlInfo/search/display/display.w3p;query=Id%3A%22legislation%2Fems%2Fr5832_ems_6286f247-9092-48bd-aac1-d771a2c7ee30%22.

European Accessibility Act (EAA). Directive (EU) 2019/882 of the European Parliament and of the Council of 17 April 2019 on the Accessibility Requirements for Products and Services (Text with EAA Relevance). European Union. Document 32019L0882. https://eur-lex.europa.eu/eli/dir/2019/882/oj.

Marrakesh Treaty to Facilitate Access to Published Works for Persons Who Are Blind, Visually Impaired or Otherwise Print Disabled, opened for signature 27 June 2013, WIPO publication; No. 218 (E). https://doi.org/10.34667/tind.28734.

The Pratt-Smooth Act (USA). Approved 3 March 1931. www.loc.gov/nls/who-we-are/laws-regulations/governing-legislation-act-march-3-1931/.

Universal Declaration of Human Rights (UDHR). United Nations, proclaimed on 10 December 1948. www.un.org/en/about-us/universal-declaration-of-human-rights

Secondary sources

Abbott, George. 2018. 'How Publishing Has Helped and Hindered Me: Experiences and Advice from a Blind Reader and Publisher'. *Learned Publishing* 31(1): 79–82. https://doi.org/10.1002/leap.1140.

AbilityNet. 2023. 'Attitudes to Digital Accessibility 2023: Survey Results and Report, October 2023'. https://abilitynet.org.uk/sites/abilitynet.org.uk/files/Attitudes-report-2023-FINAL-PDF.pdf.

Accessible Libraries. 2023. 'Creating and Editing Accessibility Metadata MARC Tags for Library Staff'. 17 October. https://accessiblelibraries.ca/resources/accessibility-metadata-for-library-staff/.

Acosta-Vargas, Patricia, Mario Gonzalez, Maria Rosa Zambrano et al. 2020. 'The Portable Document Format: An Analysis of PDF Accessibility'. In *Advances in Human Factors and Systems Interaction: AHFE 2020*, edited by Isabel L. Nunes, 206–14. Advances in Intelligent Systems and Computing, Vol. 1207. Cham: Springer. https://doi.org/10.1007/978-3-030-51369-6_28.

Adair, David, and Paul Harpur. 2019. 'Books and People with Print Disabilities: Public Value and the International Disability Human Rights Agenda'. In *The Routledge Companion to Disability and Media*, edited by Katie Ellis, Beth Haller, Rosemary Curtis, and Gerard Goggin, 400–10. *Routledge Media and Cultural Studies Companions*. New York, NY: Routledge. https://doi.org/10.4324/9781315716008-37.

ADL (Anti-Defamation League). 2017. 'A Brief History of the Disability Rights Movement'. *ADL Education*, 3 May. www.adl.org/resources/backgrounder/brief-history-disability-rights-movement.

References

Adomat, Donna Sayers. 2014. 'Exploring Issues of Disability in Children's Literature Discussions'. *Disability Studies Quarterly* 34(3). https://doi.org/10.18061/dsq.v34i3.3865.

Ahtonen, Annika, and Romain Pardo. 2013. 'The Accessibility Act: Using the Single Market to Promote Fundamental Rights'. *European Policy Centre*, 12 March. www.epc.eu/content/PDF/2013/The_Accessibility_Act.pdf.

AIPI (Australian Inclusive Publishing Initiative). 2019a. 'Inclusive Publishing in Australia: An Introductory Guide'. https://aipi.com.au/inclusive-publishing-in-australia/.

AIPI (Australian Inclusive Publishing Initiative). 2019b. 'Making Content Accessible: A Guide to Navigating Australian Copyright Law for Disability Access'. https://aipi.com.au/making-content-accessible/.

Alexander, Huw. 2022. 'Are We There Yet? The State of Accessible Publishing in 2022'. *Learned Publishing* 35(S1): 697–703. https://doi.org/10.1002/leap.1505.

Amazon. 2022. 'How Amazon Is Building a More Accessible Future'. 4 October. www.aboutamazon.com/news/devices/how-amazon-is-building-a-more-accessible-future.

APA (Australian Publishers Association). 2024. 'Diversity and Inclusion Plan'. https://publishers.asn.au/Web/Our-Work/Projects-Campaigns/DAI/Diversity-Inclusion-Plan.aspx.

Arciuli, Joanne, and Tom Shakespeare. 2023. 'Language Matters: Disability and the Power of Taboo Words'. In *The Palgrave Handbook of Disability and Communication*, edited by Michael S. Jeffress, 17–29. Cham: Springer. https://doi.org/10.1007/978-3-031-14447-9_2.

Ashwell, Sabrina J., Patricia K. Baskin, Stacy L. Christiansen et al. 2023. 'Three Recommended Inclusive Language Guidelines for Scholarly Publishing: Words Matter'. *Learned Publishing* 36(1): 94–99. https://doi.org/10.1002/leap.1527.

References

Assets'94. 1994. *Assets'94 Proceedings of the First Annual ACM Conference on Assistive Technologies*. New York: Association for Computing Machinery. https://dl.acm.org/doi/proceedings/10.1145/191028.

Association of Canadian Publishers. 2019. '2018 Canadian Book Publishing Diversity Baseline Survey'. https://publishers.ca/wp-content/uploads/2019/03/2018-Diversity-Survey-Summary-Report.pdf.

Association of Canadian Publishers and the Canadian Publishers' Council. 2023. '2022 Canadian Book Publishing Diversity Baseline Survey'. *Association of Canadian Publishers*. https://publishers.ca/wp-content/uploads/2023/02/230123-Diversity-Baseline-Survey-Report-FINAL.pdf.

Association of Canadian Publishers and eBOUND Canada. 2020. 'Accessible Publishing Research Project'. *Association of Canadian Publishers*, April. https://publishers.ca/accessible-publishing-research-project/.

Australia Reads. 2021. 'National Reading Survey: Survey Report'. https://australiareads.org.au/national-reading-survey/.

Australian Disability Network. n.d. 'Disability Statistics'. https://and.org.au/resources/disability-statistics/.

Australian Government. 2020. 'Easy Read'. *Australian Government Style Manual*. Last updated 6 September 2021. www.stylemanual.gov.au/content-types/easy-read.

Axelrod, Jamie. 2018. 'Making Materials Accessible to Students in Higher Education Institutes: Institutional Obligations, Methods of Compliance, and Recommendations for Future Action'. *Learned Publishing* 31(1): 39–44. https://doi.org/10.1002/leap.1148.

Barker, Clare, and Stuart Murray. 2018. 'Introduction: On Reading Disability in Literature'. In *The Cambridge Companion to Literature and Disability*, edited by Clare Barker and Stuart Murray, 1–14. Cambridge Companions to Literature. Cambridge: Cambridge University Press. https://doi.org/10.1017/9781316104316.002.

References

Barnes, Colin. 2020. 'Understanding the Social Model of Disability: Past, Present and Future'. In *The Routledge Handbook of Disability Studies*, edited by Nick Watson and Simo Vehmas, 14–31. New York: Routledge. https://doi.org/10.4324/9780429430817-2.

Beckett, Angharad, Nick Ellison, Sam Barrett, and Sonali Shah. 2010. '"Away with the Fairies?" Disability within Primary-Age Children's Literature'. *Disability & Society* 25(3): 373–86. https://doi.org/10.1080/09687591003701355.

Ben-Moshe, Liat. 2005. '"Lame Idea": Disabling Language in the Classroom'. In *Building Pedagogical Curb Cuts: Incorporating Disability in the University Classroom and Curriculum*, edited by Liat Ben-Moshe, Rebecca C. Cory, Mia Feldbaum, and Ken Sagendorf, 107–15. Syracuse: Syracuse University.

Bermúdez, Ana María. 2024. 'Publisher's Ownership of Accessibility'. International Publishers Association. 11 June. https://internationalpublishers.org/publishers-ownership-of-accessibility/.

Best, Krista L., W. Ben Mortenson, Zach Lauzière-Fitzgerald, and Emma M. Smith. 2022. 'Language Matters! The Long-Standing Debate between Identity-First Language and Person First Language'. *Assistive Technology* 34(2): 127–28. https://doi.org/10.1080/10400435.2022.2058315.

BISG (Book Industry Study Group). 2019. 'BISG Guide to Accessible Publishing & Cheat Sheets'. www.bisg.org/products/bisg-guide-to-accessible-publishing–cheat-sheets.

Blackham, Alysia, Lauren Ryan, and Leah Ruppanner. 2023. 'Enacting Intersectionality: A Case Study of Gender Equality Law and Positive Equality Duties in Victoria'. *Monash University Law Review* 49(3): 40–73.

Boggs, Jeff. 2010. 'An Overview of Canada's Contemporary Book Trade in Light of (Nearly) Four Decades of Policy Interventions'. *Publishing Research Quarterly* 26(1): 24–45. https://doi.org/10.1007/s12109-010-9152-9.

References

BookNet Canada. 2023. 'Podcast: Jamie Oliver Braille Publishing Milestone: Impact on Readers and the Industry'. www.booknetcanada.ca/blog/2023/12/19/podcast-jamie-oliver-braille-publishing-milestone-impact-on-readers-and-the-industry.

Bowes III, Frederick. 2005. 'Accessibility Requirements Take on New Significance for Publishers'. *Publishing Research Quarterly* 21(3): 35–45. https://doi.org/10.1007/s12109-005-0039-0.

Bowes III, Frederick. 2018. 'An Overview of Content Accessibility Issues Experienced by Educational Publishers'. *Learned Publishing* 31(1): 35–38. https://doi.org/10.1002/leap.1145.

Bradford, Anu. 2020. *The Brussels Effect: How the European Union Rules the World*. New York, NY: Oxford University Press. https://doi.org/10.1093/oso/9780190088583.001.0001.

Brady, Laura. 2024. 'The European Accessibility Act for Non-EU Members'. *International Publishers Association*, 25 March. https://internationalpublishers.org/the-european-accessibility-act-for-non-eu-members/.

Brady, Laura, and Daniella Levy-Pinto. 2019. 'Accessible Ebook Publishing in Canada: The Business Case'. *Inclusive Publishing*, 18 June. https://inclusivepublishing.org/blog/accessible-ebook-publishing-the-business-case/.

Burges, Jo. 2018. 'CAL Download: An Innovative Approach to Making Books More Accessible'. *Learned Publishing* 31(1): 57–62. https://doi.org/10.1002/leap.1133.

C4DISC (Coalition for Diversity and Inclusion in Scholarly Communications). 2022. 'Guidelines on Inclusive Language and Images in Scholarly Communication'. https://assets.pubpub.org/jcnh8c3v/71666271791414.pdf.

C4DISC (Coalition for Diversity and Inclusion in Scholarly Communications). 2023. 'C4DISC Toolkit for Disability Equity in

Scholarly Communications'. https://c4disc.pubpub.org/pub/352giuf3/release/3.

Calvard, Thomas. 2021. *Critical Perspectives on Diversity in Organizations*. 1st ed. Routledge Studies in Organizational Change & Development. New York: Routledge. https://doi.org/10.4324/9781315207131.

Carey, Kevin. 2012. 'Taking Responsibility for Accessibility: The Authorial Role in Document Creation'. In *Proceedings of the Conference Universal Learning Design, Linz 2012*, edited by Teiresias Centre of Masaryk University, Vol. 2, 9–17. Brno: Masaryk University.

Carpenter, Caroline. 2022. 'The Inklusion Guide Launches to Help Organisations Improve Accessibility'. *Bookseller*, 30 August. www.thebookseller.com/features/the-inklusion-guide-launches-to-help-organisations-improve-accessibility.

Carpenter, Todd A. 2024. 'Paywalls Are Not the Only Barriers to Access: Accessibility Is Critical to Equitable Access'. *The Scholarly Kitchen*, 7 November. https://scholarlykitchen.sspnet.org/2024/11/07/paywalls-are-not-the-only-barriers-to-access/.

Cassells, Laetitia. 2020. 'The Impact of the Marrakesh Treaty on South African Publishers'. *Publishing Research Quarterly* 37(1): 41–52. https://doi.org/10.1007/s12109-020-09775-5.

Center for Disease Control and Prevention. 2023. 'Disability Impacts All of Us'. 15 May. www.cdc.gov/ncbddd/disabilityandhealth/infographic-disability-impacts-all.html.

Cheyne, Ria. 2019. *Disability, Literature, Genre: Representation and Affect in Contemporary Fiction*. Liverpool Studies in Health, Disability, Culture and Society. Liverpool: Liverpool University Press. https://doi.org/10.2307/j.ctvsn3pp7.

Chowdhury, Radhiah. 2020. '"It's Hard to Be What You Can't See": Diversity within Australian Publishing'. *Australian Publishers Association*.

www.publishers.asn.au/Web/Web/Member-Resources/PD/BDEF-Reports/BDEF-2020.aspx.

Commonwealth of Australia. 2023. 'Royal Commission into Violence, Abuse, Neglect and Exploitation of People with Disability. Final Report: Executive Summary, Our Vision for an Inclusive Australia and Recommendations'. 29 September. https://disability.royalcommission.gov.au/publications/final-report.

Conrad, Lettie Y., and Bill Kasdorf. 2018. 'Making Accessibility More Accessible to Publishers'. *Learned Publishing* 31(1): 3–4. https://doi.org/10.1002/leap.1154.

Cooper, George, Katherine Burton, Alejandra Black et al. 2023. 'Publisher–Society Partnerships to Further Image Accessibility and Global Inclusivity in the Humanities and Social Sciences: Comparing Top-Down and Bottom-Up Approaches'. *Learned Publishing* 36(1): 58–67. https://doi.org/10.1002/leap.1535.

Cooperative Children's Book Center. 2020. 'The Numbers Are In: 2019 CCBC Diversity Statistics'. *CCBlogC*, 16 June. https://ccblogc.blogspot.com/2020/06/the-numbers-are-in-2019-ccbc-diversity.html.

Cooperative Children's Book Center. 2023a. '2022 Diversity Statistics Media Kit'. https://uwmadison.app.box.com/s/rn4ccrdx8f8a2nbbqb6spx16kxcy52r1.

Cooperative Children's Book Center. 2023b. 'How Do You Do Your Analysis – What "Counts" for Each Category?' *CCBC*, 28 July. https://ccbc.education.wisc.edu/how-we-count/.

Coser, Lewis A. 1975. 'Publishers as Gatekeepers of Ideas'. *The Annals of the American Academy of Political and Social Science* 421(1): 14–22. https://doi.org/10.1177/000271627542100103.

Couser, G. Thomas. *Vulnerable Subjects: Ethics and Life Writing*, Ithaca, NY: Cornell University Press, 2003. https://doi.org/10.7591/9781501723551.

Couser, G. T. (2018). Illness, Disability, and Ethical Life Writing. CLCWeb: *Comparative Literature and Culture*, 20(5). https://doi.org/10.7771/1481-4374.3482.

Creaser, Claire, Rachel E. Spacey, and Debbie Hicks. 2012. 'Assessing the Impact of Reading for Blind and Partially Sighted Adults'. Report to Royal National Institute of Blind People, 28 September. The Reading Agency and Library and Information Statistics Unit (LISU) Loughborough University. https://hdl.handle.net/2134/13381.

Crenshaw, Kimberlé. 1989. 'Demarginalizing the Intersection of Race and Sex: A Black Feminist Critique of Antidiscrimination Doctrine, Feminist Theory and Antiracist Politics'. *University of Chicago Legal Forum* 1989(1): 23–51. http://chicagounbound.uchicago.edu/uclf/vol1989/iss1/8.

DAISY Consortium. 2021a. 'EAA Case Study: The Netherlands'. *Inclusive Publishing*, 29 October. https://inclusivepublishing.org/blog/eaa-case-study-germany/.

DAISY Consortium. 2021b. 'EAA Case Study: Germany'. *Inclusive Publishing*, 22 November. https://inclusivepublishing.org/blog/eaa-case-study-germany/.

DAISY Consortium. 2021c. 'EAA Case Study: Italy'. *Inclusive Publishing*, 30 November. https://inclusivepublishing.org/blog/eaa-case-study-italy/.

DAISY Consortium. n.d.a. 'The Marrakesh Treaty in Action'. *Daisy.org*. https://daisy.org/news-events/articles/the-marrakesh-treaty-in-action/.

DAISY Consortium. n.d.b. 'Introduction to Inclusive Publishing'. *Inclusive Publishing*. https://inclusivepublishing.org/publisher/introduction-to-inclusive-publishing/.

DAISY Consortium. n.d.c. 'Barriers to Accessible Reading in Developing Countries'. *Daisy.org*. https://daisy.org/news-events/articles/barriers-to-accessible-reading-in-developing-countries/.

Darvishy, Alireza, Rolf Sethe, Ines Engler, Oriane Pierrès, and Juliet Manning. 2023. 'The State of Scientific PDF Accessibility in Repositories: A Survey in Switzerland'. *Learned Publishing* 36(4): 577–84. https://doi.org/10.1002/leap.1581.

Degener, Theresia. 2017. 'A New Human Rights Model of Disability'. In *The United Nations Convention on the Rights of Persons with Disabilities: A Commentary*, edited by Valentina Della Fina, Rachele Cera, and Giuseppe Palmisano, 41–59. Cham: Springer International Publishing. https://link.springer.com/chapter/10.1007/978-3-319-43790-3_2.

Drabarz, Anna Katarzyna. 2020. 'Harmonising Accessibility in the EU Single Market: Challenges for Making the European Accessibility Act Work'. *Review of European and Comparative Law* 43(4): 83–102. https://doi.org/10.31743/recl.9465.

Driscoll, Beth, and Susannah Bowen. 2023. 'Diversity and the Australian Publishing Industry: Findings from a National Workforce Survey'. *Publishing Research Quarterly* 39(4): 311–23. https://doi.org/10.1007/s12109-023-09969-7.

eBOUND Canada. 2024. 'Accessibility Metadata: Best Practices for Ebooks'. *Accessible Publishing Learning Network*, March. https://apln.ca/accessibility-metadata-best-practices-for-ebooks/.

EDItEUR. 2023. 'ONIX for Books Codelists Issue 62'. July. www.editeur.org/files/ONIX%20for%20books%20-%20code%20lists/ONIX_BookProduct_Codelists_Issue_62_Changes.pdf.

EDRLab. 2022. 'Feedback about User Experience Guide for Displaying Accessibility Metadata 1.0'. https://edition-accessible.github.io/signalement/documents/EDRLab-Signalement_lettreW3C_EN.pdf.

EducationLinks. 2019. 'Adapting eBooks for Accessibility across Open Publishing Platforms in Africa'. *USAID*, 16 April. www.edu-links.org/learning/adapting-ebooks-accessibility-across-open-publishing-platforms-africa.

Eisenstein, Elizabeth L. 1979. *The Printing Press as an Agent of Change: Communications and Cultural Transformations in Early Modern Europe*. Cambridge: Cambridge University Press.

Ellis, Katie, and Gerard Goggin. 2015. *Disability and the Media*. Basingstoke: Palgrave Macmillan. https://doi.org/10.1007/978-1-137-50171-4.

Ellis, Katie, Gerard Goggin, Beth A. Haller, and Rosemary Curtis (Eds). 2019. *The Routledge Companion to Disability and Media*. New York: Routledge. https://doi.org/10.4324/9781315716008.

European Union of the Deaf. 2022. 'Deadline for EAA Transposition Period Missed by Many EU Member States'. 30 September. www.eud.eu/deadline-for-eaa-transposition-period-missed-by-many-eu-member-states/.

Fayyaz, Nosheen, Shah Khusro, and Shakir Ullah. 2021. 'Accessibility of Tables in PDF Documents: Issues, Challenges, and Future Directions'. *Information Technology and Libraries* 40(3): 1–20. https://doi.org/10.6017/ital.v40i3.12325.

Ferri, Delia. 2020. 'The European Accessibility Act and the Shadow of the "Social Market Economy"'. *European Law Review* 45(5): 660–80.

Ferri, Delia. 2024. 'The Marrakesh Treaty to Facilitate Access to Published Works for Persons Who Are Blind, Visually Impaired or Otherwise Print Disabled in the European Union: Reflecting on Its Implementation and Gauging Its Impact from a Disability Perspective'. *IIC – International Review of Intellectual Property and Competition Law* 55(1): 89–109. https://doi.org/10.1007/s40319-023-01410-y.

Fondazione LIA. 2022. 'E-books for All: Towards an Accessible Publishing Ecosystem'. *Fondazione LIA Whitepaper*. www.fondazionelia.org/en/resources/e-books-for-all/.

Forget, Ellen, and Alex Wingate with contributions from Taylor Hare. 2024. 'Disability and Accessibility in Book Studies Bibliography'. *SHARP News*, 15 March. https://sharpweb.org/sharpnews/2024/03/

15/disability-and-accessibility-in-book-studies-sonic-electronic-and-digital-book-history-bibliographies/.

Freeman, Jason. 2022. 'SIGACCESS: 50 Years of Support Research on Accessibility in Computing'. *ACM SIGACCESS Accessibility and Computing* 132(7): 1. https://doi.org/10.1145/3523265.3523272.

Fries, Kenny. 2018. 'The Exclusivity of Inclusion: On Disability and Diversity'. *Medium*, 20 June. https://medium.com/@kennyfries/the-exclusivity-of-inclusion-on-disability-and-diversity-cc1de6d7c4b4.

Fruchterman, Jim. 2017. 'E-Books and Human Rights'. In *Disability, Human Rights, and Information Technology*, edited by Jonathan Lazar and Michael Ashley Stein, 143–57. Philadelphia, PA: University of Pennsylvania Press. https://doi.org/10.9783/9780812294095-011.

Ganner, Julie, Agata Mrva-Montoya, Maryanne Park, and Kate Duncan. 2023. 'Books without Barriers: A Practical Guide to Inclusive Publishing'. Institute of Professional Editors and the Australian Publishers Association. https://publishers.asn.au/BooksWithoutBarriers.

Gardner, John, Vladimir Bulatov, and Robert Kelly. 2009. 'Making Journals Accessible to the Visually Impaired: The Future Is Near'. *Learned Publishing* 22(4): 314–19. https://doi.org/10.1087/20090408.

Garrish, Matt. 2012. *Accessible EPUB3*. O'Reilly Media. www.oreilly.com/library/view/accessible-epub-3/9781449329297/.

Gies, Ted. 2018. 'The ScienceDirect Accessibility Journey: A Case Study'. *Learned Publishing* 31(1): 69–76. https://doi.org/10.1002/leap.1142.

Gilmore, Linda, and Glenn Howard. 2016. 'Children's Books that Promote Understanding of Difference, Diversity and Disability'. *Journal of Psychologists and Counsellors in Schools* 26(2): 218–51. https://doi.org/10.1017/jgc.2016.26.

Girma, Haben. 2016. 'A Brief Disability Accessibility Guide'. *Haben Girma*, 12 October. https://habengirma.com/2016/10/12/producing-positive-disability-stories-a-brief-guide/.

Girma, Haben. 2017. 'Break Down Disability Barriers to Spur Growth and Innovation'. *Financial Times*, 13 September. www.ft.com/content/d8997604-97ab-11e7-8c5c-c8d8fa6961bb.

Goggin, Gerard, and Christopher Newell. 2007. 'The Business of Digital Disability'. *The Information Society* 23(3): 159–68. https://doi.org/10.1080/01972240701323572.

Google. n.d. 'Accessibility: Initiatives and Research'. www.google.com.au/accessibility/initiatives-research/.

Government of Canada. 2022. 'Accessible Digital Books – Support for Organizations'. www.canada.ca/en/canadian-heritage/services/funding/book-fund/accessible-books-organizations.html.

Greco, Gian Maria. 2018. 'The Nature of Accessibility Studies'. *Journal of Audiovisual Translation* 1(1): 205–32. https://doi.org/10.47476/jat.v1i1.51.

Grigas, Vincas, and Arūnas Gudinavičius. 2023. 'Book Publishing and Print Disabilities: The Extent of Book Famine in Lithuania'. *Logos* 34(1): 61–70. https://doi.org/10.1163/18784712-03104059.

Gunn, Dave. 2016. 'Accessible eBook Guidelines for Self-Publishing Authors'. Accessible Book Consortium and International Authors Forum, January. www.accessiblebooksconsortium.org/news/en/2016/news_0002.html.

Hadley, Bree. 2022. 'A "Universal Design" for Audiences with Disabilities?' In *Routledge Companion to Audiences and the Performing Arts*, edited by Matthew Reason, Lynne Conner, Katya Johanson, and Ben Walmsley, 177–89. London: Routledge. https://doi.org/10.4324/9781003033226-14.

Hall, Frania. 2013. *The Business of Digital Publishing: An Introduction to the Digital Book and Journal Industries*. London: Taylor & Francis Group.

Haller, Beth A. 2024. *Disabled People Transforming Media Culture for a More Inclusive World*. London: Taylor & Francis. https://doi.org/10.4324/9781003219118.

Haller, Beth, Bruce Dorries, and Jessica Rahn. 2006. 'Media Labeling versus the US Disability Community Identity: A Study of Shifting Cultural Language'. *Disability & Society* 21(1): 61–75. https://doi.org/10.1080/09687590500375416.

Harkonen, Kira. 2018. 'How Do Readers Use Ebooks?' *BookNet Canada*, 1 August. www.booknetcanada.ca/blog/2018/8/1/how-do-readers-use-ebooks.

Harpur, Paul. 2017. *Discrimination, Copyright and Equality: Opening the e-Book for the Print-Disabled*. Cambridge Disability Law and Policy Series. Cambridge: Cambridge University Press.

Harpur, Paul, and Michael Ashley Stein. 2021. 'The Relevance of the CRPD and the Marrakesh Treaty to the Global South's Book Famine'. In *Accessible Technology and the Developing World*, edited by Michael Ashley Stein and Jonathan Lazar, 193–214. Oxford: Oxford University Press. https://doi.org/10.1093/oso/9780198846413.003.0010.

Hawthorne, Susan. 2014. *Bibliodiversity: A Manifesto for Independent Publishing*. North Melbourne: Spinifex Press.

Helfer, Laurence R. 2023. 'The Marrakesh Treaty: Using the Tools of Intellectual Property Law to Advance Human Rights'. In *Improving Intellectual Property*, edited by Susy Frankel, Margaret Chon, Graeme B. Dinwoodie, Barbara Lauriat, and Jens Schovsbo, 28–37. Cheltenham: Edward Elgar. https://doi.org/10.4337/9781035310869.00014.

Hendel, Richard (ed). 2013. Aspects *of Contemporary Book Design*. Iowa City, IA: University of Iowa Press.

Hilderley, Sarah. 2013 [2011]. 'Accessible Publishing Best Practice Guidelines for Publishers'. EDItEUR, WIPO and the DAISY

Consortium. www.accessiblebooksconsortium.org/publishing/accessible_best_practice_guidelines_for_publishers.

Holt, Simon, Sylvia Hunter, Erin Osborne-Martin, and Stacy Scott. 2023. 'Why Disability Data Capture Is Key to Improving Inclusion Outcomes in Scholarly Publishing'. *Learned Publishing* 36(1): 31–36. https://doi.org/10.1002/leap.1538.

House, Emma, Richard Orme, and Mark Bide. 2018. 'Towards Universal Accessibility: The UK Policy Landscape and Supporting Technology'. *Learned Publishing* 31(1): 31–34. https://doi.org/10.1002/leap.1144.

Huang, Tiffany C. T. 2023. 'Graphic Designers' Consideration of Color Accessibility'. Honours Thesis. Elon University. www.elon.edu/u/academics/communications/journal/archive/fall-2023/fall-2023-tiffany-c-t-huang/.

Hurix. 2023. 'The Business Benefits of Accessibility for Publishers'. *HurixDigital*, 22 May. www.hurix.com/business-benefits-of-accessibility-for-publishers/.

Iglesias, Violaine. 2018. 'Beyond the Mandates: The Far-Reaching Benefits of Multimedia Accessibility'. *Learned Publishing* 31(1): 49–54. https://doi.org/10.1002/leap.1153.

Inklusion Guide. 2022. www.inklusionguide.org/download.

IPEd (Institute of Professional Editors). 2024. 'IPEd Standards for Editing Practice'. www.iped-editors.org/about-editing/iped-standards/.

Jones, Alison. 2015. 'Corporate Social Responsibility in Publishing'. *BookBrunch*, 6 August. www.bookbrunch.co.uk/page/free-article/corporate-social-responsibility-in-publishing/.

Kasdorf, Bill. 2018. 'Why Accessibility Is Hard and How to Make It Easier: Lessons from Publishers'. *Learned Publishing* 31(1): 11–18. https://doi.org/10.1002/leap.1146.

Keller, Liwah. 2023. 'Improving the Right to Read in Canada: The Marrakesh Treaty, Commercial Availability and Beyond'. *Canadian*

Bar Review 101(1): 148–80. https://heinonline.org/HOL/P?h=hein.journals/canbarev101&i=148.

Kerscher, George, and Jennifer Sutton. 2004. 'DAISY for All: Publishers' Collaboration Enabling Print Access'. *Information Technology and Disabilities* 10(1). http://itd.athenpro.org/volume10/number1/kerscher.html.

Kingsbury, Margaret. 2021. 'The Current State of Disability Representation in Children's Books'. *BookRiot*, 28 April. https://bookriot.com/disability-representation-in-childrens-books.

Kleege, Georgina. 2018. *More than Meets the Eye: What Blindness Brings to Art*. New York: Oxford University Press. https://doi.org/10.1093/oso/9780190604356.001.0001.

Kleege, Georgina, and Scott Wallin. 2015. 'Audio Description as a Pedagogical Tool'. *Disability Studies Quarterly* 35(2). https://doi.org/10.18061/dsq.v35i2.4622.

Kumar, Anukriti, and Lucy Lu Wang. 2024. 'Uncovering the New Accessibility Crisis in Scholarly PDFs: Publishing Model and Platform Changes Contribute to Declining Scholarly Document Accessibility in the Last Decade'. In *The 26th International ACM SIGACCESS Conference on Computers and Accessibility* (ASSETS '24), 27–30 October, St John's, NL, Canada. ACM, New York. https://doi.org/10.1145/3663548.3675634.

Ladd, Paddy. 2003. *Understanding Deaf Culture: In Search of Deafhood*. Blue Ridge Summit: Multilingual Matters.

Lazar, Jonathan, Daniel F. Goldstein, and Anne Taylor. 2015. *Ensuring Digital Accessibility through Process and Policy*. Burlington: Elsevier Science. https://doi.org/10.1016/C2013-0-13367-3.

Lee & Bow Books. 2016. 'Where Is the Diversity in Publishing? The 2015 Diversity Baseline Survey Results'. *The Open Book Blog*, 26 January. https://blog.leeandlow.com/2016/01/26/where-is-the-diversity-in-publishing-the-2015-diversity-baseline-survey-results/.

Lee & Bow Books. 2020. 'Where Is the Diversity in Publishing? The 2019 Diversity Baseline Survey Results'. *The Open Book Blog*, 28 January. https://blog.leeandlow.com/2020/01/28/2019diversitybaselinesurvey/.

Lee & Bow Books. 2024. 'Where Is the Diversity in Publishing? The 2023 Diversity Baseline Survey Results'. *The Open Book Blog*, 28 February. https://blog.leeandlow.com/2024/02/28/2023diversitybaselinesurvey/.

Li, Jingyi, and Niloufer Selvadurai. 2017. 'Facilitating Access to Published Works for Persons with a Print Disability: Amending Australian Copyright Laws to Ensure Compliance With the "Marrakesh Treaty"'. *Monash University Law Review* 43(3): 619–47.

Library of Congress. 2009. 'Understanding MARC Bibliographic: Machine-Readable Cataloging'. 9th ed. Network Development and MARC Standards Office, Library of Congress. www.loc.gov/marc/umb/.

Linguistic Society of America. 2016. 'Guidelines for Inclusive Language'. November. www.linguisticsociety.org/resource/guidelines-inclusive-language.

Lockyer, Suzanne, Claire Creaser, and J. Eric Davies. 2005. 'Availability of Accessible Publications: Designing a Methodology to Provide Reliable Estimates for the Right to Read Alliance'. *Health Information & Libraries Journal* 22(4): 243–52. https://doi.org/10.1111/j.1471-1842.2005.00616.x. https://onlinelibrary.wiley.com/doi/abs/10.1111/j.1471-1842.2005.00616.x.

Lucas, Brian. 2020. 'Learning to Implement and Scale Up Responsible and Inclusive Business Practices'. *K4D Helpdesk Report 725*, 20 January. Brighton: Institute of Development Studies. https://assets.publishing.service.gov.uk/media/5e3c4899ed915d091ad1cae9/725_Implementing_responsible_business_practices.pdf.

Manis, Caroline, and Huw Alexander. 2018. 'The Secrets of Failing Better: Accessible Publishing at SAGE: A Case Study'. *Learned Publishing* 31(1): 63–68. https://doi.org/10.1002/leap.1138.

McNaught, Alistair, Ruth MacMullen, Sue Smith, and Vicky Dobson. 2018. 'Evaluating E-Book Platforms: Lessons from The E-Book Accessibility Audit'. *Learned Publishing* 31(1): 5–10. https://doi.org/10.1002/leap.1143.

Mellins, Simon. 2024. 'Show Me the Money: Making a Business Case for Accessibility in Small and Large Publishing Organisations'. *Book Machine*, 8 April. https://bookmachine.org/2024/04/08/show-me-the-money-making-a-business-case-for-accessibility-in-small-and-large-publishing-organisations/.

Miller, Jeffrey Archer. 2024. 'Strengthening the Rights of Persons with Disabilities in Europe to Access Goods and Services'. *European Journal of Legal Studies* 15(2): 171–211. https://doi.org/10.2924/EJLS.2024.010.

Mrva-Montoya, Agata. 2020a. 'Inclusive Publishing in Australia: A Preliminary Report'. Sydney: University of Sydney. https://doi.org/10.25910/bvmq-mk02.

Mrva-Montoya, Agata. 2020b. *Producing Accessible Books in Australia: A Snapshot*. Sydney: University of Sydney. https://doi.org/10.25910/zzws-e015.

Mrva-Montoya, Agata. 2022a. 'Towards "Born-Accessible" Educational Publishing'. *Publishing Research Quarterly* 38(4): 735–48. https://doi.org/10.1007/s12109-022-09922-0.

Mrva-Montoya, Agata. 2022b. 'How Do You Read: Key Issues and Challenges for Readers with Print Disabilities in Australia and Aotearoa New Zealand'. Presentation at the 2022 Round Table on Information Access for People with Print Disabilities. Online, 17 May.

Murray, Simone. 2020. *Introduction to Contemporary Print Culture: Books as Media*. 1st ed. London: Routledge. https://doi.org/10.4324/9780429322747.

Nankervis, Madison. 2022. "Diversity in Romance Novels: Race, Sexuality, Neurodivergence, Disability, and Fat Representation." *Publishing*

Research Quarterly 38(2): 349–363. https://doi.org/10.1007/s12109-022-09881-6.

National Council on Disability. 2004. 'Design for inclusion: Creating a New Marketplace'. Washington, DC: National Council on Disability. https://ncd.gov/publications/2004/Oct282004.

NNELS (National Network for Equitable Library Service). 2022. 'The Equitable Access to Reading Program'. *NNELS*, July. https://nnels.ca/equitable-access-reading-program.

NNELS (National Network for Equitable Library Service). n.d. 'Partnering with NNELS for Ebook Accessibility (2022–2024)'. https://nnels.ca/partnering-nnels-ebook-accessibility-2022-2024.

Nordicity and Association of Canadian Publishers. 2018. 'The Canadian English-Language Book Publishing Industry Profile: Final Report'. https://publishers.ca/wp-content/uploads/2018/11/Book-Publishing-Industry-Profile-FINAL.pdf.

Otmar, Renée. 2023. *Editing for Sensitivity, Diversity and Inclusion: A Guide for Professional Editors*. 2nd ed. Melbourne: Cambridge University Press. https://doi.org/10.1017/9781009154642.

PAAG (Publishing Accessibility Action Group). 2022. 'PAAG Survey 2022'. www.paag.uk/state-of-accessible-publishing-in-the-uk/.

PAAG (Publishing Accessibility Action Group). 2023. Publishing Accessibility Action Group Annual Report 2023.

PAAG (Publishing Accessibility Action Group). n.d. 'Business case'. www.paag.uk/business-case/.

Penrose, Rebecca Bryant. 2023. 'Normalizing Disability Using Children's Literature'. *Communication Teacher* 37(3): 171–77. https://doi.org/10.1080/17404622.2022.2162558.

Persson, Hans, Henrik Åhman, Alexander Arvei Yngling, and Jan Gulliksen. 2015. 'Universal Design, Inclusive Design, Accessible Design, Design for All: Different Concepts – One Goal? On the Concept of

Accessibility – Historical, Methodological and Philosophical Aspects'. *Universal Access in the Information Society* 14(4): 505–26. https://doi.org/10.1007/s10209-014-0358-z.

The Polish Book Institute. 2023. 'The Polish Book Market 2023'. https://instytutksiazki.pl/en/polish-book-market,7,reports,18,polish-book-market-2023,51.html.

Poynton, Scott. 2017. *Beyond Certification*. 1st ed. London: Taylor & Francis. https://doi.org/10.4324/9781351274128.

Prager, Joshua Harris. 1999. 'People with Disabilities Are Next Consumer Niche'. *Wall Street Journal* (Europe), 16 December, 4. www.wsj.com/articles/SB945213765959569213.

Publishers Association. 2019. 'Quality Control'. 31 July. www.publishers.org.uk/quality-control/.

Publishers Association. 2020. 'UK Publishing Industry Diversity and Inclusion Survey 2019'. 21 January. www.publishers.org.uk/publications/diversity-survey-of-the-publishing-workforce-2019/.

Publishers Association. 2021. 'UK Publishing Workforce 2020: Diversity, Inclusion and Belonging'. 11 February. www.publishers.org.uk/publications/diversity-survey-of-the-publishing-workforce-2020/.

Publishers Association. 2022. 'UK Publishing Workforce 2021: Diversity, Inclusion and Belonging'. 25 March. www.publishers.org.uk/publications/diversity-survey-of-the-publishing-workforce-2021/.

Publishers Association. 2023. 'UK Publishing Workforce 2022: Diversity, Inclusion and Belonging'. 31 January. www.publishers.org.uk/publications/the-uk-publishing-workforce-diversity-inclusion-and-belonging-in-2022/.

Publishers Association. n.d. 'Diversity and Inclusion'. www.publishers.org.uk/our-work/diversity-and-inclusion/.

PWDA (People with Disability Australia). 2021. 'PWDA Language Guide: A Guide to Language About Disability'. 21 August Update. https://pwd.org.au/resources/language-guide.

Riccobono, Mark A. 2015. 'Epilogue: Driving into the Future: New Paths, New Patterns, New Possibilities'. In *Building the Lives We Want: The Seventy-fifth Anniversary History of the National Federation of the Blind*, edited by Deborah Kent Stein. National Baltimore: Federation of the Blind. https://nfb.org/about-us/history-and-governance/building-lives-we-want.

Rieger, Janice, Bree Hadley, Sarah Barron, Sarah Boulton, and Catherine Parker. 2023. 'Codesigning Access: A New Approach to Cultures of Inclusion in Museums and Galleries'. In *Curating Access: Disability Art Activism and Creative Accommodation*, edited by Amanda Cachia, 183–95. Milton: Routledge. https://doi.org/10.4324/9781003171935-19.

Riley II, Charles A. 2012. *Disability and the Media: Prescriptions for Change*. Hanover: University Press of New England. https://doi.org/10.2307/j.ctv1xx9cc1.

Roberts, Nancy. 2021. 'Diversity and Inclusion in Publishing: What Do We Know?' *Publishing Research Quarterly* 37(2): 255–63. https://doi.org/10.1007/s12109-021-09805-w.

Rosen, Stephanie S. 2018. *Accessibility & Publishing*. Against the Grain, LLC, http://dx.doi.org/10.3998/mpub.10212548.

Rosenberg, Adeline, Joanne Walker, Sarah Griffiths, and Rachel Jenkins. 2023. 'Plain Language Summaries: Enabling Increased Diversity, Equity, Inclusion and Accessibility in Scholarly Publishing'. *Learned Publishing* 36(1): 109–18. https://doi.org/10.1002/leap.1524.

Round Table (Round Table on Information Access for People with Print Disabilities Inc.). 2024. 'Guidelines for Producing Accessible E-text'. https://printdisability.org/guidelines/guidelines-for-producing-accessible-etext-2024/.

Rubery, Matthew. 2016. *The Untold Story of the Talking Book*. Cambridge, MA: Harvard University Press. https://doi.org/10.4159/9780674974555.

Rubery, Matthew. 2022. *Reader's Block: A History of Reading Differences*. Stanford: Stanford University Press. https://doi.org/10.1515/9781503633421.

Saha, Anamik, and Sandra van Lente. 2020. *Re:Thinking 'Diversity' in Publishing*. Goldsmiths Press. www.spreadtheword.org.uk/wp-content/uploads/Rethinking-Diversity-in-Publishing.pdf.

Sandusky, Brett. 2012. 'User Experience, Reader Experience'. In *Book: A Futurist's Manifesto: Essays from the Bleeding Edge of Publishing*, edited by Hugh McGuire and Brian O'Leary. Boston, MA: O'Reilly Media. https://pressbooks.pub/book/chapter/user-experience-reader-experience-brett-sandusky/.

Schwarz, Thorsten, Sachin Rajgopal, and Rainer Stiefelhagen. 2018. 'Accessible EPUB: Making EPUB 3 Documents Universal Accessible'. In *Computers Helping People with Special Needs*, edited by Klaus Miesenberger and Georgios Kouroupetroglou, 85–92. Cham: Springer. https://doi.org/10.1007/978-3-319-94277-3_16.

Scott, Stacy. 2022. 'The "Long and Winding Road" for Digital Accessibility'. *Learned Publishing* 35(S1): 690–96. https://doi.org/10.1002/leap.1501.

SIDPT (Supporting {Inclusive Digital Publishing} Through Training: Questionnaire Results. 2020. 'Questionnaire Results'. *Dedicon.nl*, June. https://www.dedicon.nl/sites/default/files/2020-07/SIDPT_Questionnaire_RESULTS_report_v04.docx.

Stack Whitney, Kaitlin, Julia Perrone, and Christie A. Bhalai. 2024. 'Open Access Journals Lack Image Accessibility Guidelines'. *Quantitative Science Studies*: 6: 46–62. https://doi.org/10.1162/qss_a_00338.

Stamm, Auston, and Yu-Chang Hsu. 2021. 'The Marrakesh Treaty's Impact on the Accessibility and Reproduction of Published Works'. *TechTrends* 65(5): 692–95. https://doi.org/10.1007/s11528-021-00623-7.

Standards Australia. 2016. 'Accessibility Requirements Suitable for Public Procurement of ICT Products and Services'. Australian Standard AS EN 301 549:2016. https://store.standards.org.au/product/as-en-301-549-2016.

Suber, Peter. 2012. *Open Access*. Cambridge, MA: MIT Press. https://doi.org/10.1162/LEON_r_00535.

Suzuki, Masakazu, and Katsuhito Yamaguchi. 2020. 'On Automatic Conversion from E-Born PDF into Accessible EPUB3 and Audio-Embedded HTML5'. In *Computers Helping People with Special Needs*, edited by Klaus Miesenberger, Roberto Manduchi, Mario Covarrubias Rodriguez, and Petr Peňáz, 410–16. ICCHP 2020. Lecture Notes in Computer Science, Vol. 12376. Cham: Springer. https://doi.org/10.1007/978-3-030-58796-3_48.

Szentirmai, Attila Bekkvik, Yavuz Inal, and Anne Britt Torkildsby. 2024. 'The Accessibility Paradox: Can Research Articles Inspecting Accessibility Be Inaccessible?' *Computers Helping People with Special Needs*. ICCHP 2024, edited by Klaus Miesenberger, Petr Peňáz, and Makato Kobayashi. Lecture Notes in Computer Science, vol. 14750, 47–54. Cham: Springer. https://doi.org/10.1007/978-3-031-62846-7_6.

Taylor, Deb. 2021. 'Accessibility and Digital EPUBs'. *Publishers Weekly* 268(47), 19 November. www.publishersweekly.com/pw/by-topic/digital/content-and-e-books/article/87915-accessibility-and-digital-epubs.html.

Thompson, Arthur, and Martin Klopstock. 2023. 'Supporting an Industry-Wide Shift towards Universally Accessible Reading Experiences'. *International Publishers Association*, 11 July. https://internationalpublishers.org/supporting-an-industry-wide-shift-towards-universally-accessible-reading-experiences/.

Tink, Amanda, and Jessica White. 2023. 'Henry Lawson and Judith Wright Were Deaf – but They're Rarely Acknowledged as Disabled Writers: Why Does That Matter?' *Conversation*, 2 July. https://theconversation.com/henry-lawson-and-judith-wright-were-deaf-but-theyre-rarely-acknowledged-as-disabled-writers-why-does-that-matter-208365.

Tracy, Daniel G. 2015. 'The Users of Library Publishing Services: Readers and Access Beyond Open'. *The Journal of Electronic Publishing* 18(3): 49. https://doi.org/10.3998/3336451.0018.303.

Trimble, Lauren. 2018. 'Accessibility at JSTOR: From Box-Checking to a More Inclusive and Sustainable Future'. *Learned Publishing* 31(1): 21–24. https://doi.org/10.1002/leap.1134.

Turner, Brad. 2018. 'Benetech Global Literacy Services: Working Towards a "Born Accessible" World'. *Learned Publishing* 31(1): 25–29. https://doi.org/10.1002/leap.1141.

Tusler, Anthony. 2005. 'How to Make Technology Work: A Study of Best Practices in United States Electronic and Information Technology Companies'. *Disability Studies Quarterly* 25(2). https://doi.org/10.18061/dsq.v25i2.551.

Verboom, Maarten. 2019. 'Accessible Book Publishing, A Dutch model'. IFLA World Library and Information Congress: 'Equitable Library Services for Everybody Including Persons with Print Disabilities', Alexandria. http://library.ifla.org/2734/1/S22-2019-verboom-en.pdf.

Vleugels, Cynthia. 2021. 'The Marrakesh Treaty'. *Journal of Disability Policy Studies* 32(2): 76–82. https://doi.org/10.1177/1044207320937419.

W3C (World Wide Web Consortium). 2017. 'EPUB Accessibility 1.0'. W3C Member Submission 25 January. www.w3.org/submissions/epub-a11y/.

W3C (World Wide Web Consortium). 2021. 'User Experience Guide for Displaying Accessibility Metadata 1.0'. Final Community Group Report 27 September. www.w3.org/2021/09/UX-Guide-metadata-1.0/principles/.

W3C (World Wide Web Consortium). 2023. 'Web Content Accessibility Guidelines (WCAG) 2.2'. W3C Recommendation 5 October. www.w3.org/TR/WCAG22.

W3C (World Wide Web Consortium). 2024a. 'Accessibility Properties Crosswalk (schema.org, ONIX, MARC21 & UNIMARC)'. 19 March. https://w3c.github.io/publ-a11y/drafts/a11y-crosswalk-MARC/index.html.

W3C (World Wide Web Consortium). 2024b. 'User Experience Guide for Displaying Accessibility Metadata 2.0'. Draft Community Group Report 03 April. https://w3c.github.io/publ-a11y/UX-Guide-Metadata/draft/principles/.

W3C WAI (World Wide Web Consortium Web Accessibility Initiative). 2018. 'The Business Case for Digital Accessibility'. 9 November. www.w3.org/WAI/business-case/.

W3C WAI (World Wide Web Consortium Web Accessibility Initiative). 2021. 'Making Audio and Video Media Accessible'. 29 November, www.w3.org/WAI/media/av/.

W3C WAI (World Wide Web Consortium Web Accessibility Initiative). 2023. 'WCAG 2.1 Understanding Docs'. 20 June. www.w3.org/WAI/WCAG21/Understanding/.

Wagner, Richard K., Fotena A. Zirps, Ashley A. Edwards et al. 2020. 'The Prevalence of Dyslexia: A New Approach to Its Estimation'. *Journal of Learning Disabilities* 53(5): 354–365. https://doi.org/10.1177/0022219420920377.

WBU (World Blind Union). 2024. 'World Blind Union Statement on World Braille Day: Celebrating 200 Years of Braille'. Massachusetts Commission for the Blind. www.mass.gov/news/world-blind-union-statement-on-world-braille-day-celebrating-200-years-of-braille.

Wells Ajinkya, Ashley, Kimberly Gladfelter Graham, Alice Meadows et al. 2023. 'Implementing a Diversity, Equity, Inclusion, and Accessibility

Strategy: Lessons Learned at Five Scholarly Communications Organizations'. *Learned Publishing* 36(1): 119–23. https://doi.org/10.1002/leap.1534.

Wentz, Brian, Paul T. Jaeger, and John Carlo Bertot (Eds). 2015. *Accessibility for Persons with Disabilities and the Inclusive Future of Libraries*. Advances in Librarianship, Vol. 40. Leeds: Emerald Group. https://doi.org/10.1108/S0065-2830201540.

WHO (World Health Organization). 2019. 'World Report on Vision'. Geneva: World Health Organization. www.who.int/publications/i/item/9789241516570.

Wobbrock, Jacob O. 2019. 'Situationally-Induced Impairments and Disabilities'. In *Web Accessibility: A Foundation for Research*, edited by Yeliz Yesilada and Simon Harper, 59–92. London: Springer London. https://doi.org/10.1007/978-1-4471-7440-0_5.

Wong, Alice (ed.). 2020. *Disability Visibility: First-Person Stories from the Twenty-First Century*. New York, NY: Penguin Random House.

Wong, Alice. 2022. *Year of the Tiger: An Activist's Life*. New York, NY: Penguin Random House.

Wong, Alice. 2023. 'Disabled Authors Deserve, and Demand, More'. *Publishers Weekly*, 21 July, www.publishersweekly.com/pw/by-topic/columns-and-blogs/soapbox/article/92821-disabled-authors-deserve-and-demand-more.html.

Wong, Alice (ed.). 2024. *Disability Intimacy: Essays on Love, Care, and Desire*. New York, NY: Penguin Random House.

Wood, Laura C., Jamie Axelrod, John Stephen Downie et al. 2017. 'Libraries: Take AIM!: Accessible Instructional Material and Higher Education'. http://hdl.handle.net/10427/010667.

Yesilada, Yeliz, and Simon Harper, eds. 2019. *Web Accessibility: A Foundation for Research*. 2nd ed. Human–Computer Interaction Series. London: Springer London. https://doi.org/10.1007/978-1-4471-7440-0.

Young, Stella. 2014. 'Inspiration Porn and the Objectification of Disability'. *TEDxSydney*, 26 April. https://tedxsydney.com/talk/inspiration-porn-and-the-objectification-of-disability-stella-young/.

Yu, Zhi, Jiajun Bu, Sijie Li, Wei Wang, Lizhen Tang, and Chuanwu Zhao. 2020. 'Research on Book Recommendation System for People with Visual Impairment Based on Fusion of Preference and User Attention'. In *Computers Helping People with Special Needs*, edited by Klaus Miesenberger, Roberto Manduchi, Mario Covarrubias Rodriguez, and Petr Peňáz, 83–90. ICCHP 2020. Lecture Notes in Computer Science, Vol. 12376. Cham: Springer. https://doi.org/10.1007/978-3-030-58796-3_11.

Acknowledgements

I am grateful to all the individuals from the Australian Inclusive Publishing Initiative and the Round Table on Information Access for People with Print Disabilities who supported my learning journey, in particular Julie Ganner (Institute of Professional Editors), Sonali Marathe (NextSense), and Sarah Runcie (previously at the Australian Publishers Association). I would also like to thank Laura Brady, Gerard Goggin (Western Sydney University), John Hartley (University of Sydney), Sarah Hilderley (DAISY Consortium), Dushan Mrva-Montoya, Cristina Mussinelli and Elisa Molinari (Fondazione LIA), Jens Tröger (Bookalope), Jack Tsonis, and the anonymous reviewers for their helpful comments and suggestions on the various drafts of the manuscript. All errors are solely mine.

Cambridge Elements ≡

Publishing and Book Culture

SERIES EDITOR
Samantha J. Rayner
University College London

Samantha J. Rayner is Professor of Publishing and Book Cultures at UCL. She is also Director of UCL's Centre for Publishing, co-Director of the Bloomsbury CHAPTER (Communication History, Authorship, Publishing, Textual Editing and Reading) and co-Chair of the Bookselling Research Network.

ASSOCIATE EDITOR
Leah Tether
University of Bristol

Leah Tether is Professor of Medieval Literature and Publishing at the University of Bristol. With an academic background in medieval French and English literature and a professional background in trade publishing, Leah has combined her expertise and developed an international research profile in book and publishing history from manuscript to digital.

ADVISORY BOARD

Simone Murray, Monash University
Claire Squires, University of Stirling
Andrew Nash, University of London
Leslie Howsam, Ryerson University
David Finkelstein, University of Edinburgh
Alexis Weedon, University of Bedfordshire
Alan Staton, Booksellers Association
Angus Phillips, Oxford International Centre for Publishing
Richard Fisher, Yale University Press
John Maxwell, Simon Fraser University
Shafquat Towheed, The Open University
Jen McCall, Central European University Press/Amsterdam University Press

About the Series

This series aims to fill the demand for easily accessible, quality texts available for teaching and research in the diverse and dynamic fields of Publishing and Book Culture. Rigorously researched and peer-reviewed Elements will be published under themes, or 'Gatherings'. These Elements should be the first check point for researchers or students working on that area of publishing and book trade history and practice: we hope that, situated so logically at Cambridge University Press, where academic publishing in the UK began, it will develop to create an unrivalled space where these histories and practices can be investigated and preserved.

Cambridge Elements ≡

Publishing and Book Culture

The Business of Publishing

Gathering Editor: Rachel Noorda

Dr Rachel Noorda is the Director of Publishing at Portland State University. Dr Noorda is a researcher of twenty-first-century book studies, particularly on topics of entrepreneurship, marketing, small business, national identity, and international publishing.

ELEMENTS IN THE GATHERING

Entrepreneurial Identity in US Book Publishing in the Twenty-First Century
Rachel Noorda

Is This a Book?
Angus Phillips and Miha Kovač

Are Books Still 'Different'? Literature as Culture and Commodity in a Digital Age
Caroline Koegler and Corinna Norrick-Rühl

China's eBook Evolution: Disruptive Models and Emerging Book Cultures
Xiang Ren

Behaviour Beyond the Text and the Morality Clause in Twenty-First-Century Publishing
Chiara Bullen

Inclusive Publishing and the Quest for Reading Equity
Agata Mrva-Montoya

A full series listing is available at: www.cambridge.org/EPBC

Made in the USA
Monee, IL
03 May 2026